Fusion \ 'fyü zhen\ n. :

a merging of diverse, distinct, or separate elements into a unified whole

Resurrections

\ rĕz' ə rĕk' shəns \ n. :

a theme throughout Scripture

by Joshua D. Genig

I0794808

CONCORDIA PUBLISHING HOUSE • SAINT LOUIS

3558 S. Jefferson Ave., St. Louis, MO 63118-3968
1-800-325-3040 • www.cph.org

Written by Joshua D. Genig
Edited by Mark S. Sengele

This publication may be available in braille, in large print, or on cassette tape for the visually impaired. Please allow 8 to 12 weeks for delivery. Write to Lutheran Blind Mission, 7550 Watson Rd., St. Louis, MO 63119-4409; call toll-free 1-888-215-2455; or visit the Web site: www.blindmission.org.
Your comments and suggestions concerning the material are appreciated. Please write the Editor of Youth Materials, Concordia Publishing House, 3558 S. Jefferson Avenue, St. Louis, MO 63118-3968.
Manufactured in the United States of America

Table of Contents

INTRODUCTION

About the Fusion Series

Fusion—the merging of diverse, distinct, or separate elements into a unified whole. Fusion is a word that speaks of energy and excitement, whether you are talking about a style of music or a nuclear reaction.

God's Word is filled with fusion. The Old Testament bears many hints of events to come in the New Testament, yet we often miss the connection. The Gospel message of the Savior is seen time and again in the Old Testament. Through this series you will come to connect—fuse—those events and messages for yourself and your participants.

Each study in the Fusion Series gathers stories from Scripture—both Old and New Testaments—around a common theme. Our prayer is that, through the study of that theme, you will come to a deeper understanding of the Gospel message of Jesus Christ as Lord and Savior.

Fusion—Resurrections

Throughout all of Holy Scripture, there is an overarching theme of death versus life. Often, this is played out in the physical sense. People die and people are given new life, or resurrected. Moreover, the theme of death versus life finds its culmination in the death and resurrection of Jesus Christ. He is forsaken by His Father and killed in the body. He is loved by the Father and raised in the body.

However, each instance of death versus life also has a deeper meaning. There is not only a battle between physical death and life but also between spiritual death and life. Every biblical example of death with an ensuing resurrection serves to prefigure what has happened to every Christian. All human beings are spiritually dead, yet in Jesus Christ and the incorporation into His death and resurrection, those once dead human beings are resurrected and made Christians. This transferal from the realm of death to the realm of resurrection is the mark of every Christian only because it was first the mark of Christ!

Using These Materials

Fusion Series Bible studies are designed to challenge your participants to develop a deeper knowledge and understanding of Scripture. These studies work for either large-group presentation or small-group Bible study. While there are six sessions outlined in the book, there are no suggested time limits for each section of the lesson. The level of participant interest, discussion, and further questions will help establish the length of time to spend on each section. This flexibility also allows you to use this material for more than six one-hour sessions. You can easily adapt this material to twelve or more hour-long lessons.

Each session contains reproducible participant pages. These pages may be given to participants as you work through the lesson together in class. As an alternative, you may give copies of these pages to participants in advance of the session so that they may complete their personal study before coming to class.

The leader's materials work through the questions from the participant pages and provide additional commentary and insights for the Bible class leader. You will want to study these notes as you prepare to lead each session.

It is assumed that the Bible class leader will have the usual basic equipment and supplies available—pencils or pens for each participant and a chalkboard or its equivalent (white board, overhead transparency projector, or newsprint pad and easel) with corresponding markers or chalk. Encourage the participants to bring their own Bibles. Then they can mark useful passages and make notes to guide their personal Bible study and reference. Do provide additional Bibles, however, for visitors or participants who do not bring one. The appropriate participant pages should be copied in a quantity sufficient for the class.

1

Isaac

Lesson Focus

"God will provide for Himself the lamb for a burnt offering, my son" (Genesis 22:8).

Before the foundation of the world, God saw the corruption that would come of His creation, "and mindful of His mercies great, He planned for my salvation" ("Dear Christians, One and All, Rejoice," *LSB* 556:4; *LW* 353:4).

Gospel Focus

God's plan was never to abandon His creation, but rather, to send His own dear Son, Jesus Christ, to be the Lamb of God who takes away the sin of the world (John 1:29). Although God's plan came to fruition many years after it first began, a great number of individuals along the way looked quite similar to the one God had promised. More than any other, though, Isaac prefigured this Lamb to come. The similarities are most clearly seen in Isaac's near sacrifice, where he even carried his own wood to the place of his near death. In faith, Isaac was spared—resurrected to new life—while a ram in the thicket took his place as the burnt offering.

Prayer

O God of all grace, You sent Your Son, our Savior Jesus Christ, to bring life and immortality to light. We give You thanks that by His death He destroyed the power of death and by His resurrection He opened the kingdom of heaven to all believers. Strengthen us in the confidence that because He lives we shall live also, and that neither death nor life nor things present nor things to come will be able to separate us from Your love which is in Christ Jesus our Lord, who lives and reigns with You and the Holy Spirit, one God, now and forever (*LSB Agenda*, p. 121).

Introduction

What does it mean to make a promise? What are some major promises (or vows) that people typically make? What are the implications of weighty promises like these? How are they remembered?

Read Genesis 3:15. What promise does God make in this verse? Who is the fulfillment of this promise? What other promises of God do you remember from the Old Testament? What comfort can we find in God's promises today?

God is in the business of making promises. In fact, He has been ever since the very beginning. After the transgression of our first parents, Adam and Eve, God began to make promises that would change the course of the world forever. Adam and Eve had just begun to adjust to their new wardrobe of fig leaves, with their fingers still pointing at anyone from spouse to serpent, and God was already bringing about His plan of salvation. God said to the serpent, "I will put enmity between you and the woman, and between your offspring and her offspring; He shall bruise your head, and you shall bruise His heel" (Genesis 3:15). The "He" of this promise is none other than God's very own Son, Jesus Christ.

All of God's promises are centered on Jesus Christ and the redemption won for us by Him. However, there would be many more years and many more promises before the "He" of Genesis 3:15 actually broke onto the scene to take on our very flesh and blood. At times, the fulfillment of God's promises seemed quite unlikely. It would have taken just one false swing of the sword or one angry ruler, and any key link in the "salvation chain" could have been broken. This fact was never clearer than it was with Isaac. But we shall see that God does not lie. Although many generations passed from the fall of man into sin until the incarnation, when God became man, God's promise of a Savior remained sure. He was faithful and He would do it!

Believe It or Not?

Read Genesis 17:15–21; 18:1–15; and 21:1–7. Why are Abraham and Sarah unusual candidates to become parents? God makes Abraham another promise in these verses. What is unusual about this promise? How do Abraham and Sarah react to God's promise? How would you react?

It is hard to believe God would carry out His promise of a Savior through a couple as old as Abraham and Sarah. It was bad enough that Sarah was barren—not able to have children. One strike against them! Moreover, when God promised a child to Abraham and Sarah, he was one hundred years old and she was ninety years old. It would seem highly unlikely that anyone that age could bear a child, let alone care for them for many years to come. Two strikes against them! One more and someone's out!

Read Luke 1:37. Here, Luke relates the story of another individual facing an unusually similar situation to that of Abraham and Sarah. What is the promise made to this individual? How does she react? Compare this story with Abraham and Sarah.

Yet, "nothing will be impossible with God" (Luke 1:37). Barrenness and old age are no match for the One who created the world with His Word and man and woman from dust and a rib. His plan to send the Savior of the world would not be changed by the effects of the fall. It was, of course, God's intention that man and woman be fruitful and multiply (Genesis 1:28). However, with the fall into sin, things were dramatically changed. Creation was flawed. Relationships were flawed. Bodies were flawed. Yet, with His promise of a Savior, God was beginning to bring all of fallen creation under a new head, His own Son, Jesus Christ. No longer would people be ruled by the sin that once condemned them. Under their new head, people would be brought back to the way things were in Eden. No sin. No death. Perfect creation. Perfect relationships. Perfect bodies.

But for the time being, Abraham lived in reality. He only knew this fallen creation. He knew his wife was barren. He knew they were too old to have children. So one can surely imagine how outrageous the news of the impending arrival must have sounded to him. It was enough to send him falling on his face in laughter. Yet this laughter was not intended to mock God. It is not as though Abraham was thinking, Yeah right! You're going to give my old, barren wife a child. We'll see about that. No, it was not like that at all. Rather, this was joyful laughing that was caused by God Himself. In fact, it is quite similar to the laughter that God *made* for Sarah (21:6) after the birth of this promised child, Isaac.

Promises Fulfilled

What connections do you begin to see between Isaac and Jesus? What does this reveal about how God chooses to make and keep His promises?

To whom does all of Holy Scripture point? Why do you think He stands at the center of everything?

The birth of Isaac was nothing short of a miracle. God said, "Sarah your wife shall bear you a son, and you shall call his name Isaac" (Genesis 17:19). As if that was not enough, He went on to say, "I will establish my covenant with him as an everlasting covenant for his offspring after him" (17:19). The Lord visited Sarah, and the promise became flesh and dwelt among us (Genesis 21:2). Sarah bore her beloved husband a son.

By now, the deep connection between Isaac and Jesus can already be seen. Both were the children promised by God. Both were born to unsuspecting mothers, with Sarah being barren and Mary a virgin. The news of both births caused great rejoicing; Abraham fell on his face with laughter, and Mary, having consented, sang her joyous hymn of praise (the Magnificat). But if these were the only connections between Isaac and Jesus, one could likely chalk it up to mere coincidence. Yet there is always more when it comes to the Scriptures, because every last letter is there to bear witness to Jesus the Christ (John 5:39). As Luther so brilliantly said, "The entire Scripture deals only with Christ" (AE 25:405); moreover, "All the stories of Holy Writ, if viewed aright, point to Christ" (AE 22:339).

You Want Me to Do What?

What happens when a promise is broken? What are some ways that people react to broken promises? How would you react if a significant promise made to you was broken? How is the promise-breaker seen afterwards?

Most people react to broken promises by becoming upset and even angry. Students may share a variety of reactions that they may have had when a promise made to them was broken. A person who breaks their promise is often viewed with contempt or distrust.

In Genesis 22:2, how does God seemingly break His promise to Abraham? What might Abraham be thinking, especially after the emotional events surrounding the birth of this boy? How does Abraham react? Compare this to Abraham's reaction in Genesis 17.

It would have been hard enough to imagine that God would grant a child to a barren couple in their old age. Yet, it is even harder to imagine that God would then ask Abraham to sacrifice this promised child. Not only would He be taking away a long-awaited child, but He would be destroying the everlasting covenant He made through Isaac. Sadly, it appears as if God is a liar. Not only will His promise fail, but He is the one causing its failure.

It is not hard to imagine how anyone other than Abraham would have reacted to God's request. Anyone else would probably begin by pointing fingers and yelling, "But You promised!" Anyone else would have called God out and attempted to negotiate with Him or make demands of Him. Anyone else, especially a loving father, would probably have offered up his own life in place of his son's.

Strangely enough, though, Abraham did not do any of these things. He did not argue with God. He did not badger God. He did not even question God. He did not disobey God. Never once did he say, "You want me to do what?" Just as Abraham did not react with doubt at the announcement of his wife's conception in her barren old age, but rather rejoiced in faithfulness, he once again did not doubt or question, but was completely faithful to the will of God. Therefore, when Abraham was told to sacrifice his only son, the promised child of the covenant, he did not even hesitate. Abraham "rose early in the morning, saddled his donkey, and took two of his young men with him, and his son Isaac" (Genesis 22:3). To the world, Abraham appears to be a delinquent father, but to our Father in heaven, he is wholly faithful. In likeness to Mary once more, it was almost as though Abraham gave his own silent version of "Behold, I am the servant of the Lord; let it be to me according to Your word" (Luke 1:38).

As Good as Dead

Can you think of anyone else who was led to his death? Can you imagine knowing you would have a loved one die in just a few days? In what ways does Isaac being led look like Jesus on "the way of sorrows"?

Expand your list of similarities between Isaac and Jesus. What do we learn about Jesus from Isaac at this point?

It was not a quick journey to the land of Moriah. In faithfulness, Isaac's face was set by his father toward the place of his death (Luke 9:51). For three days, Isaac and Abraham journeyed to that mountain. For three days, they made their way to the place of his slaughter. Yet, for anyone who was not there, it is nearly impossible to imagine those three tormenting days. What did they discuss? Were there any tears? Yes, Isaac was alive and well, but he had a death sentence placed on him. It would not be long before that healthy boy would be dead and burned to ashes.

Oftentimes, when death is imminent, and there is no chance of recovery or turning back, it is almost as though death has already occurred. A person diagnosed with terminal cancer and in hospice care, with only weeks to live, may appear to those around them to have already given up their life. They have lost their freedom. Death is certain. It is as if it had already happened. This is not unlike Jesus walking to His death. When Jesus was on the way of sorrows, and almost to the cross, no bystander could rejoice in the few hours He had left. Rather, beaten and battered, it was as though He was already dead. In fact, Jesus was so brutally beaten and tortured, many who loved Him probably wanted Him to get to Golgotha as quickly as possible. He would surely die, and in their minds, He was already as good as dead.

Chances are it was a bit like that for Abraham. There was no doubt in his mind that his son would be killed. He was not hoping for another way. Abraham was not hoping that God would change His mind. He was just hoping to get there and do what God had asked of him. In Abraham's mind, his son was already as good as dead, and it was just a matter of time before his life would end. Although Isaac may not have known the fullness of God's request, he was certainly a dead man walking for *three days*.

Finally, Isaac's own way of sorrows was complete, as "Abraham lifted up his eyes and saw the place from afar" (Genesis 22:4). The place of death was now in full view. No turning back! Isaac bore the wood of his death (John 19:17) as he and his father finished their three-day journey. He took the final steps to the holy mountain, where he would be slain at God's command.

Something's Not Right

Read Genesis 22:4–8. What does Isaac notice is missing for this offering? Explain Abraham's response to Isaac. What does he mean in verse 8? How does Abraham's answer to Isaac's question show you Jesus Christ?

Take a moment to imagine the emotions between father and son in these brief verses. What must Abraham be thinking? What must Isaac be thinking? Where is faith in these excruciating moments?

As Abraham and his beloved son, Isaac, made their way to the place of his death, with wood on back, and fire and knife in hand, something appeared to be missing. Isaac recognized that this sacrifice was not like any he had ever seen before. They had three out of four ingredients for a sacrifice, but one crucial thing was missing, the lamb to be slaughtered. As Isaac so innocently said, "Behold, the fire and the wood, but where is the lamb for a burnt offering?" (Genesis 22:7). Or as the hymn "The Lamb" (*LSB* 547; *HS98* 822) says, "The Lamb, the Lamb, O Father where's the sacrifice? Faith sees, believes, God will provide the Lamb of price!"

Who is that Lamb of price? Was Abraham banking on the fact that God would send a lamb and spare his son? At first glance it surely seems that way. To Isaac's innocent question, Abraham responded, "God will provide for Himself the lamb for a burnt offering, my son" (Genesis 22:8). Abraham appears to gently console his son with the assurance that God would provide a lamb and his son would not be killed. But that really doesn't fit with all that has been said about Abraham's faithfulness to God's command. If Abraham was faithful, he would not have hoped for a way out of killing his son. He would not have hoped for a lamb to take the place of Isaac on the altar lit with flame. Rather, he had every intention of doing the deed and turning his son to ashes.

With that in mind, it is clear that when Abraham said, "God will provide for Himself the lamb for a burnt offering, my son" (Genesis 22:8), that lamb was none other than his own son, Isaac. These words of Abraham were not meant to console his son, but they were words of truth. It was not as though Abraham was saying, "I know you're a bit scared, but don't worry. A lamb will die in place of you, my dear son." No, Abraham was fully intent on sacrificing his own son at the will of God. These words of Abraham should be understood as Abraham saying, "God will provide the lamb . . . and you, *my son*, are it!"

Does this sound a bit familiar? Well, it certainly should! In Abraham's willingness to kill his own son, he prefigures the willingness of the Father to sacrifice His own Son, Jesus Christ. Abraham, like our Father in heaven, knew there was no other way, that His own beloved Son "must suffer many things and be rejected by the elders and chief priests and scribes, and be killed, and on the third day be raised" (Luke 9:22). There was no way out. Salvation would only come through the death of the new and greater Isaac. If Abraham does not kill his son, he denies the will of God. If our Father in heaven does not kill His Son, He denies His creation and is made to be a liar. Therefore, Abraham calling his son "the lamb" is absolutely crucial to understanding the mission and work of Jesus Christ, since the one who provides the true Lamb is the Father, and that Lamb is His beloved Son!

Read John 10:14–18. How does Isaac's willingness to lay down his life foreshadow the willingness and authority of Jesus to lay down his life?

As often as we've read these verses, we are often pointed to the faithfulness of Abraham and his trust in the Lord. What about Isaac? Put yourself in his shoes. What other options does he have? In what ways does Isaac show even greater faithfulness? Again, how does this point us to Jesus?

Often, people feel bad for Isaac because he appears to be coerced into laying down his life. Luther, however, estimates that Isaac was around twenty years of age when his father led him to his sacrifice. Other theologians have speculated that Isaac was anywhere from twenty-five to thirty-seven. The point to be made is that this was not some young child, totally helpless and dependent upon his father, who was being lured away to his death. Rather, with Abraham at around one hundred twenty years of age, and his son a young man, Isaac probably could have ended this excursion at any point with brute strength and youth alone. Yet, "like a lamb that is led to the slaughter, and like a sheep that before its shearers is silent, so he opened not his mouth" (Isaiah 53:7; Acts 8:32). It is Isaac who lays down his life of his own accord, for he alone has "authority to lay it down" (John 10:18). The faithfulness of Abraham is matched by the faithfulness of his son, Isaac. But what was the driving force behind Abraham's faithfulness, and Isaac's for that matter? What would allow a father to sacrifice his son? What would allow a son to be bound to an altar and burned to ashes? What would allow a person to obey the will of God, even unto death?

What is hope? Who has hope in these verses? What is our hope as Christians?

Being faithful unto death is completely dependent upon whether or not a person has hope. If there is no hope, there is no faithfulness. Abraham and Isaac can be faithful only on account of the hope they possess. This hope is very concrete and clearly seen by the instruction Abraham gave to the two young men who accompanied them on the journey to Moriah. Abraham said to them, "Stay here with the donkey; I and the boy will go over there and worship and come again to you" (Genesis 22:5). Catch that? Not "I will come again to you," but "I and the boy will . . . come again to you."

Abraham's hope cannot be seen as unwillingness to sacrifice his own son. As far as Abraham was concerned, there was no backing out. But there was hope! Not hope that God would provide an animal, since Isaac was that lamb. Rather, his hope was that God was faithful and would not lie. Isaac was the promised child of Abraham and Sarah. He was conceived by God in the womb of one who should not have been pregnant. He was the child through whom God's everlasting covenant would be established (Genesis 17:19). He was a key link to the Messiah to come, Jesus Christ. Therefore, Abraham was firmly convinced that God, who said, "Through Isaac shall your offspring be named" (Genesis 21:12), would not lie, nor void

His promise. Therefore, though Isaac be killed, God would raise him from the dead, so as to not break His promise. Luther put it beautifully when he wrote:

> *All people can see death, and the heathen and the ungodly realize that death is death. But this is the wisdom of Christians and the unique teaching of the church—the teaching to which Abraham holds fast: "Though I am killing my son, I have him alive." And Isaac: "Though I die, I shall not die when you cut my throat and reduce me to ashes. To be sure, I shall be turned to ashes. Nevertheless, I shall live, and I shall beget heirs of the entire world."*
> (AE 4:118)

This is true hope. This is true faith. Abraham believed God. He believed his son could not be killed forever. He believed he would bear offspring and remain the child of the covenant. Thus Abraham could make that long walk to his son's death. He believed in the resurrection!

Caught in the Act

Think about what you have learned about sacrifice in the Bible. Animals were the victims of sacrifice on behalf of the people. How does the meaning of the sacrifice change when it is a human being? Does the idea of human sacrifice fit with the pictures of Abraham and Isaac you were shown in Sunday School? What sacrifice does this ultimately prepare us for?

"When they came to the place of which God had told him, Abraham built an altar there and laid the wood in order and bound Isaac his son and laid him on the altar, on top of the wood. Then Abraham reached out his hand and took the knife to slaughter his son" (Genesis 22:9–10). Abraham functioned as priest and bound his son, Isaac, to the altar like any other sacrificial animal. The altar had been built. The wood was arranged. Abraham had his knife ready. The sacrificial rite is about to begin.

At this point, it is nearly impossible to picture the scene. It is grotesque and brutal in nature and is even more dreadful because it is a loving father who is ready to slit the throat of his own son. Yet there were no second thoughts. Abraham was not pacing around the altar trying to find another way. Abraham was obedient to God. Isaac was obedient to his father. With his knife to the throat of his son, the only thing that could halt the impending sacrifice was the voice and intervention of God Himself.

"But the angel of the Lord called to him from heaven and said, 'Abraham, Abraham!' And he said, 'Here am I.' He said, 'Do not lay a hand on the boy or do anything to him'" (Genesis 22:11–12). Here, God's intervention is often thought of as a voice from the clouds. Historically, though, artwork has portrayed this intervention by the angel of the Lord as an angel actually grabbing the arm of Abraham as he moves to slit the throat of his dear son. The point is that it was more than a quiet voice of the angel of the Lord telling Abraham to stop the sacrifice; it was the angel of the Lord actually *preventing* Abraham from killing Isaac. Although this scene looked as though it would end with bloodshed and smoke rising to the heavens, it did not. God broke onto the scene and acted on behalf of his children by stopping Abraham from doing the unthinkable—killing his own dear son.

Discuss how Abraham's true hope was in the Christ to come. How does his naming of that place support this hope?

"And Abraham lifted up his eyes and looked, and behold, behind him was a ram, caught in the thicket by his horns" (Genesis 22:13). Yes, God sent a ram, a male lamb, to die in the place of Isaac. For that reason, "Abraham called the name of that place, 'The Lord will provide'; as it is said to this day, 'On the mount of the Lord it shall be provided'" (Genesis 22:14). The Lord provided, and Abraham named the place as such. But he did not give it that name merely because of the male lamb who died in his son's place. Rather, there would come a time when a man about Isaac's age would be brought to His own sacrificial altar. This new and greater Isaac, Jesus Christ, would be led to His slaughter, bearing the wood of His cross. But in this case, God had no choice but to abandon His own dear Son, the Lamb of God, on the cross, free of any angel's intervention.

The holy Lamb undaunted came
To God's own altar lit with flame;
While weeping angels hid their eyes,
This Priest became a sacrifice.
("The Infant Priest Was Holy Born," *LSB* 624:3; *HS98* 853:3; © 1997, 2003 Chad L. Bird. Used by permission.)

By the mercy of God, Abraham was spared from killing his own son, and Isaac remained alive. "For now I know that you fear God, seeing you have not withheld your son, your only son, from Me" (Genesis 22:12). Although the angel forbade Abraham to kill his own son, his willingness to do so was as good as the deed itself. He had essentially offered up Isaac as a pleasing sacrifice to God, who in his great mercy raised him from the dead and pointed their eyes to the true Lamb. As Luther asserts, the literal translation of "On the mount of the LORD it shall be provided" is actually "On the mount the LORD will be seen" (AE 4:138). And so He has been! The Lord has been seen in the very Lamb of God who died on the mountain of Golgotha.

Dead, but Alive . . . in Christ

Read Hebrews 11:17–19. What does the writer to the Hebrews show us is the focus of Abraham's faith? By believing in the resurrection of his son, Abraham points to a greater belief in the resurrection of the Messiah. For Christians living after the Messiah has come, to what hope do these verses from Hebrews point us?

Abraham was faithful to God in offering up his son as a sacrifice, only because he had hope in the resurrection of the dead. As the writer to the Hebrews said, "He considered that God was able even to raise him from the dead, from which, figuratively speaking, he did receive him back" (Hebrews 11:19). Luther brought out this "resurrection hope" of Abraham and Isaac in his Genesis commentary when he wrote:

When Isaac's throat was about to be cut, he thought: "Into Thy hands I commit my spirit (Psalm 31:5). I shall not die, but I shall live; and I shall return, because God will not lie. I am the son of the promise. Therefore, I must beget children, even if heaven collapses." Consider whether this is not dying a sure death and nevertheless living a surer life. Hence the prophets in Holy Scripture everywhere proclaim the resurrection of the dead, and this passage clearly points out a resurrection even into this physical life. How much more into the future life! (AE 4:118–119)

Why are resurrections at the heart of our faith? (Think back to where we began with Adam and Eve.) Why is the resurrection of Jesus the most important for Christians? Where do you fit into the resurrection? What does the resurrection mean for your faith?

In the resurrection, death is vanquished. It is ended. It has no power over human beings. Yes, it will still affect creation. People will still die. But the resurrection makes right that which once went wrong. Adam and Eve sinned, and death was the necessary consequence of that transgression. Yet, in Jesus Christ, who is the Gospel promise of Genesis 3:15, God begins to make right all that which once went wrong. The final step in reversing the great curse of Adam and Eve was the bitter suffering and death, and glorious resurrection, of Jesus Christ. His cross and empty tomb stand at the center of salvation history—the only hope of a bodily resurrection for His creation is in Him. If it were not for Jesus some two thousand years after Abraham nearly slaughtered his son, Isaac's resurrection would not be possible. Apart from Jesus and His own resurrection, death has a deadly sting that no one can ever survive.

Abraham, however, believed in the Lamb to come, the one who would be sent from the Father to bruise the deadly serpent's head (Genesis 3:15). This Lamb was Jesus Christ. With unimaginable similarity to Isaac, Jesus Christ would come as the unblemished Lamb of God who takes away the sin of the world (John 1:29). Bearing His own wood, this unblemished Lamb of God willingly went forth to His own sacrificial altar at the cross. It is not merely coincidence that Abraham named that altar on Mount Moriah "the LORD will provide" (Genesis 22:14), or better translated, "the LORD will be seen." Geographically speaking, Mount Moriah was the place that would later be known as Golgotha, or the place of Jesus' crucifixion. For on that mountain, the Lord would be seen in a sacrifice far more gruesome than that of Isaac.

Mount Golgotha was the place to which the unblemished Lamb of God set His face (Luke 9:51), but, all along the way, that Lamb never opened His mouth. He never cried out in mistrust. Rather, He was completely faithful to His Father in heaven and His plan to redeem all of creation. The great Lutheran hymn writer Paul Gerhardt magnificently brought out the imagery of Jesus Christ as the Lamb of God going off to His slaughter:

A Lamb goes uncomplaining forth,
The guilt of sinners bearing
And, laden with the sins of earth,
None else the burden sharing;
Goes patient on, grows weak and faint,
To slaughter led without complaint,
That spotless life to offer,
He bears the stripes, the wounds,
the lies,
The mockery, and yet replies,
"All this I gladly suffer."
("A Lamb Goes Uncomplaining Forth,"
LSB 438:1; *TLH* 142:1)

However, that Lamb would not remain dead forever. Three days later, on the eighth day, the day of the new creation, Jesus Christ, the crucified Lamb of God, rose from the dead, victorious over death and the grave. In His resurrection, He gave meaning and certainty to all other resurrections, even Isaac's.

Icons of the resurrection of Jesus often include Him reaching out His hand to pull Adam back into the life he and his beloved lost in the Garden of Eden. Some, however, go a step further and include the patriarchs in the icon. The inclusion of Abraham and Isaac in an icon of the resurrection is for no other reason but to show that their hope has been confirmed and made sure in the resurrection of Jesus Christ. St. Paul declared, "If Christ has not been raised, then our preaching is in vain and your faith is in vain" (1 Corinthians 15:14). But thanks be to God, Christ has been raised. Abraham's faith was not in vain. Isaac's faith was not in vain. The faith of the Christian is not in vain. Since Christ was raised from the dead, so was Isaac. Since Christ was raised from the dead, so also will all Christians be.

Conclusion

Who is the new and greater Isaac? When you read the account of Isaac and his sacrifice on Mount Moriah, what mountain should you be thinking of? Who was sacrificed there?

As shown, the death and resurrection of Isaac have no meaning apart from Jesus Christ. In his very being, Isaac is a type or foreshadowing, and Jesus is the fulfillment of that type. Therefore, this account directs our eyes to no one other than Jesus Christ. He is the Paschal Lamb who went to the slaughter, but was not rescued by an angel of the Lord. He is the Paschal Lamb who took the place of Isaac and all others who deserve to die a gruesome death. He is the Paschal Lamb who willingly bore on His shoulders, not only His own cross, but also the sins of the world. In His death and resurrection, all people are given new life—the assurance of a resurrection from the dead.

God has provided the Lamb, His Son, and when one looks to Isaac and his near sacrifice, they ought to see the altar of the cross on Mount Golgotha and the Lamb of God who takes away the sin of the world hanging there for our salvation. Isaac was the lamb of his father's slaughter, but Christ is the proper Paschal Lamb. For it is in nothing other than the bitter suffering and death and victorious resurrection of the proper Paschal Lamb, Jesus Christ, that all other lambs, including Isaac, have life!

Prayer

O God, since You promised faithful Abraham that he would be the father of a great multitude, You provided a substitute for his son, Isaac. In the fullness of time, You sent Your Son, the Lamb who takes away the sin of the world, to lay down His life that we might live as faithful children of Abraham. Grant to all people a living trust in Your mercy; through Jesus Christ, our Lord. (Collect for the Easter Vigil, *LSB Lectionary: Series C,* p. 173)

ISAAC

Introduction

Discuss what it means to make a promise. What are some major promises (or vows) that people typically make? What are the implications of weighty promises like these? How are they remembered?

Read **Genesis 3:15**. What promise does God make in this verse? Who is the fulfillment of this promise? What other promises of God do you remember from the Old Testament? What comfort can we find in God's promises today?

Believe It or Not?

Read **Genesis 17:15–21**; **18:1–15**; and **21:1–7**. Why are Abraham and Sarah unusual candidates to become parents? God makes Abraham another promise in these verses. What is unusual about this promise? How do Abraham and Sarah react to God's promise? How would you react?

Read **Luke 1:37**. Here, Luke relates the story of another individual facing an unusually similar situation to that of Abraham and Sarah. What is the promise made to this individual? How does she react? Compare this story with Abraham and Sarah.

Promises Fulfilled

What connections do you begin to see between Isaac and Jesus? What does this reveal about how God chooses to make and keep His promises?

To whom does all of Holy Scripture point? Why do you think He stands at the center of everything?

You Want Me to Do What?

What happens when a promise is broken? What are some ways that people react to broken promises? How would you react if a significant promise made to you was broken? How is the promise-breaker seen afterwards?

In **Genesis 22:2**, how does God seemingly break His promise to Abraham? What might Abraham be thinking, especially after the emotional events surrounding the birth of this boy? How does Abraham react? Compare this to Abraham's reaction in **Genesis 17**.

As Good as Dead

Can you think of anyone else who was led to his death? Can you imagine knowing you would have a loved one die in just a few days? In what ways does Isaac being led look like Jesus on "the way of sorrows"?

Expand your list of similarities between Isaac and Jesus. What do we learn about Jesus from Isaac at this point?

Something's Not Right

Read **Genesis 22:4–8**. What does Isaac notice is missing for this offering? Explain Abraham's response to Isaac. What does he mean in **verse 8**? How does Abraham's answer to Isaac's question show you Jesus Christ?

Take a moment to imagine the emotions between father and son in these brief verses. What must Abraham be thinking? What must Isaac be thinking? Where is faith in these excruciating moments?

Read **John 10:14–18**. How does Isaac's willingness to lay down his life foreshadow the willingness and authority of Jesus to lay down His life?

As often as we've read these verses, we are often pointed to the faithfulness of Abraham and his trust in the Lord. What about Isaac? Put yourself in his shoes. What other options does he have? In what ways does Isaac show even greater faithfulness? Again, how does this point us to Jesus?

What is hope? Who has hope in these verses? What is our hope as Christians?

Caught in the Act

Think about what you have learned about sacrifice in the Bible. Animals were the victims of sacrifice on behalf of the people. How does the meaning of the sacrifice change when it is a human being? Does the idea of human sacrifice fit with the pictures of Abraham and Isaac you were shown in Sunday School? What sacrifice does this ultimately prepare us for?

Discuss how Abraham's true hope was in the Christ to come. How does his naming of that place support this hope?

Dead, but Alive . . . in Christ

Read **Hebrews 11:17–19**. What does the writer to the Hebrews show us is the focus of Abraham's faith? By believing in the resurrection of his son, Abraham points to a greater belief in the resurrection of the Messiah. For Christians living after the Messiah has come, to what hope do these verses from Hebrews point us?

Why are resurrections at the heart of our faith? (Think back to where we began with Adam and Eve.) Why is the resurrection of Jesus the most important for Christians? Where do you fit into the resurrection? What does the resurrection mean for your faith?

Conclusion

Who is the new and greater Isaac? When you read the account of Isaac and his sacrifice on Mount Moriah, what mountain should you be thinking of? Who was sacrificed there?

8

Ezekiel's Vision of Dry Bones

Lesson Focus

Ezekiel is called to stand in the Lord's stead and speak His life-giving Word. Without someone speaking that life-giving Word, the dry bones have no hope of new life.

Gospel Focus

"The word of God is living and active, sharper than any double-edged sword, piercing to the division of soul and spirit, of joints and of marrow" (Hebrews 4:12). Moreover, it has the power to give "soul and spirit, joints and marrow" back to the driest of dead bones. This vision of Ezekiel is truly one where creation is being made new as those dead bones receive flesh and new life and resurrection.

Prayer

Come, Holy Ghost, Creator blest,
And make our hearts Your place of rest;
Come with Your grace and heav'nly aid,
And fill the hearts which You have made.

Your light to ev'ry thought impart,
And shed Your love in ev'ry heart;
The weakness of our mortal state
With deathless might invigorate.

Drive far away our wily foe,
And Your abiding peace bestow;
With You as our protecting guide,
No evil can with us abide.

Teach us to know the Father, Son,
And You, from both, as Three in One
That we Your name may ever bless
And in our lives the truth confess.
("Come, Holy Ghost, Creator Blest,"
LSB 498/499:1, 4–6)

Introduction

Why is the vision of dry bones an odd choice for a reading on Pentecost Sunday? Read Acts 2:1–36. What is celebrated on Pentecost Sunday? Now read John 6:63, the explanation of the Third Article of the Apostles' Creed,

and questions 157–161 from Luther's Small Catechism. What is the work of the Holy Spirit? After reading these, discuss whether or not Ezekiel 37 is an appropriate reading for Pentecost Sunday.

Ezekiel, the prophet-priest, originally preached a message of Law and condemnation upon the people of Israel. Yet after Jerusalem and the temple were no more, Ezekiel's message became fully saturated with the Gospel. It is within this later matrix of hope and consolation that one will find the vision of dry bones. What is unique about the account of Ezekiel's vision is that it appears in the Church Year on Pentecost Sunday—Series B.

The Feast of Pentecost seems a peculiar place for this text to be found. What do dried-up bones that receive flesh and blood and come to life again have to do with Pentecost? Everything! This connection becomes very clear when one remembers the presence and work of the Holy Spirit prior to the Day of Pentecost. Certainly, just as Jesus was present and active before His incarnation, the Holy Spirit had an active role to play before the outpouring on the fiftieth day after Easter. As Genesis 1:2 declares, "And the Spirit of God was hovering over the face of the waters." The Holy Spirit is an integral part of creation, as nothing the Godhead does can ever be attributed to any less than all three persons (Father, Son, and Holy Spirit). The Spirit was working at creation, giving life out of nothing, and that is precisely what He does in the account of Ezekiel's vision of dry bones!

The Lord's Man

Read 1 Timothy 4:14 and 2 Timothy 1:6. Pastors are ordained and put into the Lord's service through the laying on of hands. How did Ezekiel receive his own "laying on of hands"?

Read Ezekiel 37. The laying on of hands is a sacred act for a sacred task. What is that task for Ezekiel? He is given two "words" to speak (one binds and one loosens). What are those two words? How does he preach the Law?

Contrast Ezekiel 7 with Ezekiel 37. Which one is a message of death and which is one of life? Is there a difference between the two in tone or intention?

Ezekiel begins his account with the phrase "The hand of the LORD was upon me" (Ezekiel 37:1). This is not to say the Lord's hand literally reached down from heaven and rested upon Ezekiel. Rather, this is what theologians like to call an "anthropomorphism." In other words, God takes on human characteristics or attributes, like having a hand and placing it upon someone. What the prophet is saying is that he has the Lord with him, as his task is to stand in God's stead and speak His Word.

One cannot make light of the Lord's hand. The hand of the Lord can bring judgment and destruction (see Exodus 9:3) just as easily as it can bring mercy and peace (see Acts 11:21). Moreover, the Lord's hand is laid upon those He places into His service as a mark or sign of their being made pastors. Luther says, "Thus the imposition of hands is not a tradition of men, but God makes and ordains ministers" (AE 5:249). Even here, in Ezekiel 37, the Lord is making for Himself a minister whose task is to resurrect these dead bones. By the Lord laying His hand upon him, He is assuring all that it is no longer Ezekiel who speaks or acts, but his is "the mouth and hand of God" (AE 5:249).

The significance of "The hand of the LORD" being upon Ezekiel and the task he is then given cannot be underestimated. The *Apology of the Augsburg Confession* says it this way:

> *For the ministry of the Word has God's command and has glorious promises. . . . "So shall My word be that goes out from My mouth; it shall not return to Me empty, but it shall accomplish that which I purpose" (Isaiah 55:11). If ordination is understood in this way, neither will we refuse to call the laying on of hands a Sacrament.* (Apology XIII 11–12)

The laying on of hands is certainly not a new thing. In fact, before Moses died, how did he appoint Joshua to stand in his stead as the voice of the Lord? By laying his hands on him! Moses wrote in Deuteronomy 34, "And Joshua the son of Nun was full of the spirit of wisdom, for Moses had laid his hands on him" (v. 9). The hands conveyed the spirit of wisdom needed for the task of standing in the Lord's stead and speaking His Word. Those whom the Lord calls into service are given that burdensome task of faithfully speaking His Word—Law and Gospel. This is why the Holy Ministry is also called the "Office of the Keys," as pastors are endowed with the keys to lock heaven to the unrepentant and unlock heaven to those who repent by speaking a word of Law (locking heaven) or Gospel (unlocking heaven). Ezekiel is certainly no different. The "hand of the LORD" is upon Ezekiel and the "Spirit of the LORD" aids him in his task of being pastor for the Lord and for those he is called to shepherd, even if they be dead bones!

Like the last great prophet, John the Baptizer (see Luke 1:66), Ezekiel is the Lord's man who has the task of uttering words of judgment and also words of comfort and consolation, of Law and of Gospel. However, this task is too much for any human being, and must be done with the aid and guidance of the Holy Spirit. Therefore, it is the Lord who leads him and it is the Lord who will speak through him. As he mentioned a few chapters ago, "And the Spirit of the LORD fell upon me, and He said to me, 'Say, Thus says the LORD'" (Ezekiel 11:5). Ezekiel is caught up in the Lord's doing, and in the process will be sent to one of the most undesirable of places.

Oh, the Places You'll Go!

Read Luke 3:4–5. What task is John the Baptizer given to do? How does Ezekiel's task prefigure that of John? How does a valley symbolize death, and why would it need to be raised up?

Compare the pastors of the Church with Ezekiel. How do they resemble this great prophet-priest? Think hands, spirit, task, words, and resurrection!

So, doing the Lord's work and speaking for Him, Ezekiel is brought "in the Spirit of the LORD" to a lifeless valley "full of bones" (Ezekiel 37:1). Ezekiel is like John the Baptizer in that he is given the task of speaking for the Lord; he is also brought to a valley that, by definition, is anything but level ground. Valleys are gravelike and therefore symbolize death. Remember John's task given him from Isaiah 40, "Prepare the way of the LORD, make His paths straight. Every valley shall be filled, and every mountain and hill shall be made low" (Luke 3:4–5). What's the problem with valleys? "The way that John prepares for Jesus, the Messiah, will be made straight by filling in the valleys . . . The Messiah must enter His holy city unimpeded and accomplish His destiny" (*Luke 1:1–9:50* by Arthur A. Just Jr., p. 151). How are the valleys to be filled in? The valleys are raised by John's preaching of repentance for the forgiveness of sins in preparation for the Christ. Why is John to preach this message of repentance, raising up valleys and the like? So that "all flesh shall see the salvation of God" (Luke 3:6). Through John's making the way straight for Jesus, Christ will be able to go to the cross and do His Father's bidding. In turn, all flesh will see their salvation as they gaze upon the very Lamb of God, slain on the altar of the cross in the holy city of Jerusalem.

Ezekiel's task is nearly identical to John's. He is to prepare the way for Christ to break onto the scene with His good gifts of life and resurrection and, in turn, "all flesh shall see the salvation of God." But strangely enough, flesh is precisely the thing that Ezekiel does not see in this valley of dry bones. It is his task to raise up these dry bones from the valley of sin and death, and speak a word that clothes them with flesh so they can eagerly anticipate the salvation from God in the person of Jesus Christ. Both Ezekiel and John the Baptizer share the same task—to show people Jesus!

The Dryness of Death

Discuss the reasons why water is essential to life. Given the necessity of water, how do David's words in Psalm 22 show Jesus to be the icon of dryness and death?

Before these people can see Jesus, they must first be alive. Right now, they are completely dead. Not only are the bones in a valley, symbolizing the depth of sin and the brokenness of the human heart, but they are also "very dry" (Ezekiel 37:2). The psalmist puts a voice to the lament of Jesus, "My strength is dried up like a potsherd, and My tongue sticks to My jaws; You lay Me in the dust of death" (Psalm 22:15). Jesus, merely through the lack of water and the ensuing dryness, is in and of Himself the icon of death, since it is clear that lack of water leads to death and is a clear indication of death. There is no water in these "very dry" bones, and probably has not been for quite some time. They are dead, to be sure! What do they need? True water!

Imagine Jesus' looking at His fallen creation. How does what He would see compare to what Ezekiel does see in those "very dry" bones? Do either of them see life?

Is it realistic to think that dried-up bones, residing in a valley grave, can ever come back to life?

After leading Ezekiel through all the bones (Ezekiel 37:2), giving him an excellent view of the magnitude of death, the Lord then asks a very peculiar question: "Son of man, can these bones live?" (v. 3). There are two very interesting things to note here. First, the Lord addresses Ezekiel as the "Son of man," which is a title used in the Gospels, but only comes from the lips of Jesus in reference to Himself (*Just*, p. 225). This is Jesus' way of "making a (thinly veiled) claim to be God" (*Just*, p. 229). Therefore, it is quite interesting that the Lord uses this title to address Ezekiel. This is not to say that Ezekiel is God, but, by him, the hearer should have a picture of Jesus. In other words, Ezekiel, by the very nature of what he is about to do as prophet and priest of God most high, is giving a picture or foretaste of the God-man to come, whose passion and death will bring true life, Jesus Christ.

Read Revelation 7:9–17 and Ezekiel 37:1–3. Compare and contrast these two visions. How are they similar? How are they different?

Discuss a time when you were so awestruck that what was very apparent was still quite unbelievable. (E.g., A child turns sixteen years old, and his parents buy him a car for his birthday. However, when he first sees it, he is so overwhelmed that the parent says, "Do you know whose car this is?")

The second interesting thing to note is the ridiculous question the Lord asks Ezekiel, "Can these bones live?" Certainly, dead things cannot live again, especially when they are very dead. However, the question addressed to Ezekiel is not, "Can you make these bones live?" but "Can these bones live?" The "do-er" of the actions of salvation, like living and seeing and believing, is always the Lord. Although Ezekiel, in and of himself, cannot bring life to anything that is dead, he knows full well that the Lord can. For this reason he says, "O Lord GOD, you know" (v. 3). At first glance, Ezekiel appears to dodge the question by putting it back on the Lord. In fact, a similar pattern is seen in the account of John's vision in Revelation 7.

After beholding the great multitude worshiping Christ, the Lamb of God (vv. 9–12), the account continues:

> *Then one of the elders addressed me, saying, "Who are these, clothed in white robes, and from where have they come?" I said to him, "Sir, you know." And he said to me, "These are the ones coming out of the great tribulation. They have washed their robes and made them white in the blood of the Lamb."*
> (vv. 13–14)

One must ask why the elder, or saint in heaven, even poses the question. Dr. Louis Brighton in his commentary on Revelation answers that question this way:

> *Of course the elder himself knows, for he, together with the other twenty-three [elders], represents all the saints before God's heavenly throne* (4:4)*. One would have expected John to have asked the question. . . . He was perhaps so awestruck by the appearance of the great crowd in heaven that he had said to himself, "Who are these?" The elder then sensing John's private wonder asked the question for him in 7:13. John responded, "My lord, You—You know"* (7:14). (p. 196)

In a similar fashion, Ezekiel is perhaps so awestruck over the view of all the dry, dead bones that the Lord asks the question that he is already thinking. Not sure what to answer and seeing the great feat ahead in order to make those bones actually come back to life, he responds by saying, "O Lord GOD, You know." Like the elder in Revelation, the Lord God begins to describe what is lying before Him—dry bones that will live again!

John in Revelation sees a multitude of the living and cannot believe his eyes. Ezekiel sees a multitude of the dead, and likewise, cannot believe his eyes. Ironically enough, these dead bones will soon become living bodies, quickly changing the scene to one quite similar to John in Revelation, where only life abounds. This prophet-priest, Ezekiel, stands in the stead of Jesus Himself ("son of man"), and is now about to speak words of life and immortality that will resurrect these dead bones into "a great multitude" (Revelation 7:9) who will know the Lord and worship Him as His faithful people.

Not only does the structure of the question in Ezekiel 37 point one to the resurrected ones in Revelation 7, but it also prefigures the unity of God's people (i.e., His Church). It is no mistake that John sees a multitude. Who makes up that multitude?

They are the ones who were once buried in the dryness of death, but are now resurrected and washed (remember the need for something to quench the dryness) in the blood of Jesus.

In the Lord's Stead

Read Luke 10:17. When a pastor speaks to his flock, whose voice is actually heard? Look at the Absolution in the Divine Service. In whose "stead" is the pastor standing and speaking and acting?

If Christ is the Word of God (John 1:1), and Ezekiel speaks that Word, then who do those dry bones hear?

Compare the cosmic nature of what ensues following Ezekiel's speaking and that which comes from Jesus' speaking at the cross on Good Friday.

Ezekiel, by his very call, is "watchman for the house of Israel" (Ezekiel 3:16), and his job is to speak for the Lord in His stead and by His command (see Ezekiel 2:1–3:12). Therefore, the Lord says to him:

> *Prophesy over these bones, and say to them, O dry bones, hear the word of the* Lord. *Thus says the Lord God to these bones: behold, I will cause breath to enter you, and you shall live. And I will lay sinews upon you, and will cause flesh to come upon you, and cover you with skin, and put breath in you, and you shall live, and you shall know that I am the* Lord. (Ezekiel 37:4–6)

Ezekiel is the Lord's man who does not speak his own words, but only speaks the words given him by the Lord. The Lord could easily have said to Ezekiel, "The one who hears you hears Me" (Luke 10:16). Ezekiel is not condemning or forgiving on account of his own right, but he is conveying the speech and will of God. He is the Lord's man who has the keys to bring death or life, but only utters what heaven has already declared. To whom is Ezekiel to speak? He is to speak to the dead that they might hear the Word, who is, according to John 1:1, Jesus Himself. The people are not to hear Ezekiel, but rather the true giver of life, Jesus Christ.

So Ezekiel prophesies just as the Lord told him to do, and as he does "there was a sound, and behold, a rattling, and the bones came together, bone to bone" (Ezekiel 37:7). When Ezekiel speaks, things happen. He speaks and there is a "rattling," or more appropriately, an "earthquake." When Ezekiel speaks to the dead bones, the cosmos is shaken. The world reacts to the voice of the Lord through the man He has appointed to speak for Him. In a similar way, the cosmos is shaken when the Son of Man, Jesus Christ, does His speaking from the cross. The skies darken, the temple curtain is torn in two, the earth is shaken, and the dead come up out of their tombs (see Matthew 27:45–54). The cosmic event that accompanies Ezekiel's words is a picture of what will happen at the cross, when Jesus speaks for the life of the world.

New Creations

When the bones finally received sinews, flesh, and skin, were they complete? Read Genesis 2:1–7. What completes a person? What do these bones still need?

When the *ruach* is breathed into the newly created bodies, what will they become? Discuss how this is a return to the Garden of Eden, where the breath of God created Adam. When the Lord makes things new, how does He do it? Does He destroy what was and start over, or does He take what is there and re-create it?

As Ezekiel speaks the Word of the Lord, those dead, dried-up bones receive a new start. They are no longer bones residing in a valley looking "very dry." Now they are given sinews, flesh, and skin. What once bore the marks of death are now icons of life. By the word of Ezekiel, these dead bones are resurrected and given a new start. When the Lord meets death, new lives and new beginnings are bound to prevail, for that is all that the Lord brings to the table. These dead bones are new creations because they are remade into what they once were, healthy human beings, because, when the Lord speaks, things happen!

Even amid the grandeur of new sinews, flesh, and skin, however, there is still one thing missing: breath. Breath is what is needed to complete these new creations. Without breath, they are but flesh and bone, but with the breath, they are God's own. Therefore, the Lord says to Ezekiel, "Prophesy to the breath . . . Come from the four winds, O breath, and breathe on these slain, that they may live" (Ezekiel 37:9). The bodies were created first, but a lack of "breath" is reminiscent of Genesis 2. One will recall that "the LORD formed the man of dust from the ground" as His first action and then completed that man by breathing "into his nostrils the breath of life" (v. 7). That is what makes a "living creature": body and soul, not one or the other. Commenting on Genesis 2:7 and the "breath of life" being breathed into Adam, Luther says:

> *I believe that God made the whole man from the dust of the earth, for the text [Genesis 2:7] says that God made man. "Man" doesn't mean the body alone but always means the body and the soul, and accordingly the Scriptures call the soul "the breath of life" [Genesis 2:7].*
> (AE 54:401)

Ezekiel is speaking for Jesus, so when he speaks, he speaks realities. "Behold, I will cause breath to enter you" Ezekiel says, and it happens. The Hebrew word here for "breath" is the same word for "spirit" (*ruach*). *Ruach* is breath or spirit in the sense that it animates or brings to life.

The word for breath in Genesis 2:7 is different from that in Ezekiel 37:5. In Genesis 2:7, Moses employs the word *nephesh*, which means "one's life or soul." In other words, "the breath of life" breathed into Adam (*nephesh*) means that the fullness of him was given by God. How do the two words for breath (*ruach* and *nephesh*) fit together? Simply put, Adam became a whole person, body and soul, or *nephesh*, because he received the *ruach*, the animating, life-giving Spirit of the Lord.

Therefore, it is more than mere breath that enters those bones as Ezekiel speaks things into being. Rather, the very life-giving Spirit that was breathed into Adam in the Garden of Eden, making him a whole person (*nephesh*) is re-breathed into these dead bones, essentially creating them new and whole once again (*nephesh*). It is the breath of God and the breath of God alone that brings life. It brings life because the breath of God is the very Spirit of God who is the conveyer of the new creation of body and soul. Jesus Himself says in His bread of life discourse that it is "the Spirit who gives life" (John 6:63)—and so He does!

The "very dry" bones are now living creatures, as Ezekiel speaks a life-giving word that re-creates them. In essence, what went wrong, terribly wrong, in Eden and destined all people for death is now re-created in Garden-of-Eden-like fashion as the *ruach* is breathed into these newly formed bodies. Notice, the Lord does not destroy His original creation and start over from scratch. Rather, He takes what went wrong (sinful humans who died) and re-creates them, or, in other words, resurrects them. To be sure, re-creation is nothing less than resurrection!

Who Are These?

There is often an attempt among Christians to not look "weird" or "too Christian." But do the baptized look different than non-Christians? How so?

How is the "new look" for those former bones a picture of what happens to dead sinners who are baptized?

Think back to the comparison between Ezekiel's vision and John's vision in Revelation. John sees the faithful who are "coming out of the great tribulation. They have washed their robes and made them white in the blood of the

Lamb" (Revelation 7:14). Those who John sees do not look like they did before their Baptism. Before, they were like dry bones, who rested in the valley of death. Yet now they are alive and newly created "in the blood of the Lamb." In a similar way, Ezekiel now also sees the newly created. Although they are still dry bones, the Lord tells him that those he sees as new creations "are the whole house of Israel" (Ezekiel 37:11). They are the chosen people of God, who were dead in their sins but are shown to Ezekiel to now be resurrected to new life by the Word of the Lord.

Ezekiel speaks once more, "Thus says the Lord GOD: Behold, I will open your graves and raise you from your graves, O My people. And I will bring you into the land of Israel" (Ezekiel 37:12). The Lord will empty the graves of His chosen people, now dead but soon to be alive. Moreover, He will take their resurrected bodies and place them back where they belong, Israel. Thus far, all those dead bones have known is exile from their homeland. They are foreigners and are dying away from the only place they know. Yet the Lord promises to raise their bodies and bring them back to Israel, that they might live where they belong. These chosen people are "to believe that they shall go home again" (*AE* 35:283).

They Know the Lord

Many people think that they can know God through nature or by signs and wonders. Read John 3:1–2. Nicodemus does not get it right because he only knows Jesus as the wonder worker who is "a teacher come from God" (v. 2). This is not how the Lord would have you know Him, but how would He? Where does the Lord reveal who He really is and what His ultimate purpose is?

Discuss a time when you've been away from home. Why is it often very comforting to return home? Wouldn't you like a home you'd never have to leave?

After bringing His chosen people from death to life by giving them body and soul and raising them from their graves, the Lord says that they will know Him (Ezekiel 37:13–14). How will they know Him? Certainly not by signs and wonders, for that is not how the Lord desires to be known. This is the case when Jesus meets Nicodemus in John 3, and Nicodemus falsely identifies Him as "a teacher come from God" (v. 2). Why? Because "no one can do these signs that You do unless God is with him" (v. 2). Catch that? Nicodemus believes that Jesus is a "teacher" because of His "signs" or miracles. But that is not how Jesus would like people to know Him. Not as a wonder worker or as a bread king. Rather, Jesus would have people know Him in the event that epitomizes His purpose: death and resurrection. This is why the confession of the centurion in Mark's Gospel is so glorious: "Truly this man was the Son of God" (Mark 15:39). How does he know this? By Jesus' bitter suffering and death—and the resurrection to come will only solidify it!

These dried-up bones will know the Lord because He will bring them from death to life, and He will do so by the Holy Spirit. "And I will put My Spirit within you, and you shall live" (Ezekiel 37:14). This is why this text is read on the Feast of Pentecost. Even before Jesus sent the Holy Spirit in Acts 2 (vv. 1–4), He sent Him into those dry bones through the voice of His past, Ezekiel. The hymn "Come, Holy Ghost, Creator Blest" (*LSB* 498/499; *TLH* 233) is traditionally sung on the Feast of Pentecost and throughout the Pentecost season. Its words bring out the fullness of the Spirit's job—to create and sustain new life by a living faith!

Thankfully, when the Lord promises to do something, He always comes through. He cannot and does not lie. His Word is truth (John 17:17) and will never fail. The Lord will raise up His chosen people from the graves of death unto a new life. He will resurrect Israel and bring them back to their homeland to live forever, and that is how they will know Him: by death and resurrection!

The New House of Israel

Read 1 Peter 2:1–12. Why is the message of St. Peter a fitting one for the newly baptized? Who is the new Israel? What have those newly baptized just entered into?

Since Israel and the Lord were as close as a husband and wife, discuss the idea that what happens to Israel will necessarily happen to Jesus and vice versa. Have you ever known of a spouse who suffers because the other spouse is suffering? Often, what happens to one spouse determines what will happen to the other.

Why does the Church look like Christ? How do the people of the Church reflect the vision of dry bones? Who raised our dried-up, dead bodies to new life?

St. Peter says: "But you are a chosen race, a royal priesthood, a holy nation, a people for His own possession" (1 Peter 2:9). This sermon of St. Peter is likely one preached to the newly baptized at the Vigil of Easter (Holy Saturday). But they are Christians, right? How are they a chosen race, a royal priesthood, and so forth? What about Israel? Certainly, Israel was the chosen people of God. When the Lord was doing the choosing, He chose Israel first! However, they would not have Him, so now there is a new Israel, a new people of God. This new Israel is the holy Christian Church.

The Church is the beloved bride of Jesus Christ (see Ephesians 5) and part of His own body. Nothing happened by chance in the Old Testament; everything had a purpose. For instance, the trials and tribulations of Israel happened to them, the chosen people, because of what would one day happen to Christ. They are truly one flesh! Therefore, the history of God's people determines the future of Christ (what happens to the wife happens to the husband) just as much as the future of Christ determines the history of God's people (what happens to the husband happens to the wife). Since everything that happened to Israel would one day happen to Christ, they appear to be one and the same person. However, Israel would not have the Lord. They divorced themselves from the Lord of life and salvation. Therefore, the Lord chose a new people to be His bride, a new Israel. The new chosen race is the holy Christian Church, who, being one flesh with Jesus, appears to be one and the same as Him. Simply put, when one sees the Church, the chosen people of God, they should see Christ! One cannot help but remember the hymn stanza which beautifully conveys the message of the new Israel:

Church of God, elect and glorious,
Holy nation, chosen race;
Called as God's own special people,
Royal priests and heirs of grace:
Know the purpose of your calling,
Show to all His mighty deeds;
Tell of love that knows no limits,
Grace that meets all human needs.
("Church of God, Elect and Glorious," by James E. Seddon, *LSB* 646:1*; HS98* 864:1)

Although the new chosen people are called "the Church," nevertheless they look quite similar to Israel, especially the Israel that Ezekiel sees in his vision. Like that Israel, the Church was at one time dead. As St. Paul writes to the Christians in Ephesus, "And you were dead in the trespasses and sins in which you once walked, following the course of this world, following the prince of the power of the air, the spirit that is now at work in the sons of disobedience" (Ephesians 2:1–2). The word that St. Paul uses for "dead" is *nekros*. This word brings with it the force of rotting, decomposing, stinky roadkill, absolutely unable to bring themselves back from the dead. Sounds a bit like bones that are "very dry," does it not? Completely dead! No chance of coming back to life unless someone brings resurrection!

Yet St. Paul continues by saying: "But God, being rich in mercy, because of the great love with which He loved us, even when we were dead in our trespasses, made us alive together with Christ" (Ephesians 2:4–5a). Catch that? Once as dead as a carcass on the side of the road . . . or dead bones lying in a valley . . . but now made alive with Jesus. How does this happen? All by the breath, or the Spirit, of God! As Luther says, "The bond uniting the Christian community was rather the bond that was welded by the Holy Spirit Himself" (AE Companion, Volume: 198).

Dry Bones Given the Water of Life!

Why do some not see the Sacraments in the Gospel of John? How are their misunderstandings cleared up? Read John 3:1–8; 4:13–14; 6:22–59; and 19:31–37. Now do you see them? The Sacraments are seen in the water, bread, and blood of John's Gospel.

By what means does the Holy Spirit convey the gift of life and resurrect our dead souls? When the Holy Spirit battles the demonic forces that reside in dead sinners, who is bound to win?

Creation was completed in seven days, but what happened to that creation? Why is the number eight a significant number?

Discuss what happens at the baptismal font. How does God use water to give His gift of new life and resurrection, and also quench the thirst of our dried up souls?

The Spirit of God brings life and immortality, making even the driest of bones into a living house called the Church. But how is that breath or that Spirit given? Where does He work?

Throughout the Gospels, and especially in the Gospel of John, water finds a unique place. Since John has no "official" institution of Baptism (as the others do) many often think that his Gospel is nonsacramental. However, if one looks at all the occurrences of water and how it is used, it is clear that John does not lack the Sacraments, but fully displays them as the life-giving gifts of God. It is by water that the Spirit of God works and is given. So what does water have to do with the Church being the new Israel? Everything!

Like the Israel in Ezekiel's vision, all who are dead in sin are dried up and lying in the valley of death. However, it is the life-giving Spirit of God who brings life to those dead souls through water, the one thing that quenches the thirst of all dry, dead sinners. This is why Jesus says to the woman from Samaria, "Whoever drinks of the water that I will give him will never be thirsty forever. The water that I will give him will become in him a spring of water welling up to eternal life" (John 4:13–14). That is right! The water that flows from Christ is life-giving and thirst-quenching. The water that Jesus gives is the water of Baptism.

In Holy Baptism, water is connected with God's divine name, and it becomes living water that brings life to all those upon whom it is poured. So when a child or adult comes to the font, they come as nothing short of dry bones dead in sin. Yet when they are baptized with the living water and enter the body of Jesus (this is the reference to "kingdom of God" in John 3:5) they are raised to new life—they are resurrected! How? The same Spirit who breathed into Adam in the garden and into those bones in Ezekiel comes to the font and blows the breath of life into dead sinners and brings life to their souls. Just as the Pentecost hymn declares:

> *Come, Holy Ghost, Creator blest,*
> *Vouchsafe within our souls to rest;*
> *Come with Thy grace and heav'nly aid*
> *And fill the hearts which Thou hast made.*
> ("Come, Holy Ghost, Creator Blest,"
> *LSB* 498/499:1; *TLH* 233:1)

In Luther's baptismal rite found in the Small Catechism and *Lutheran Service Book*, there is an exorcism that reads: "Therefore, depart, you unclean spirit, and make room for the Holy Spirit in the name of the Father and of the + Son and of the Holy Spirit" (*LSB Agenda*, p. 13). All demonic forces and "unclean spirits" are sent away, and the Holy Spirit makes room for

Himself and enters in, bringing with Him life and immortality! Either a person is as dead as those dry bones or resurrected like Christ, for it is all or nothing with the Holy Spirit. Thankfully, when His name is attached to water at Baptism, it is always life and resurrection that wins the day.

In the Sacrament of Holy Baptism, the Spirit is conveyed through the Word of God connected with the water. This certainly brings life and resurrection, as it is a Sacrament that re-creates fallen sinners. The number for new creation is eight, and so it is fitting that traditional baptismal fonts have eight sides, signifying that all dead sinners who pass through the water emerge on the other side as new creations. Why are they new creations? They are new creations because they are re-created just as Adam and all his children (which includes all people!) were originally created: with the breath of God. At the holy font, God breathes His own life-giving breath into dead sinners through that living water (see stanza 2 of Martin Franzmann's hymn "Thy Strong Word," *LSB* 578; *LW* 328). Just as the Spirit "was hovering over the face of the waters," so He still hovers over the font and works by the water. In turn, those whom the Spirit has resurrected and newly created are given the assurance of Eden once again—that is, heaven itself!

The Dwelling Place of the Saints

The resurrected in Ezekiel 37 were promised a home. Where is the home of those resurrected in the font?

All those who have been remade, re-created, in the waters of the font through the breath of the life-giving Spirit now are brought into a community. Just as the Lord promised to put the people of God in their own land (Ezekiel 37:14), so, too, He has put all baptized Christians in their own land: the Church. The Church is the land of the faithful because that is the place where the Christ comes to His people and cares for them with His holy Sacraments and life-giving Word. This is the new Jerusalem, as this is the place where the faithful gather to receive the fruits of the ultimate sacrifice for sin, the death of Jesus Christ and His holy body and blood. This is also the promised land, as the place where the faithful gather "with angels and archangels and with all the company of heaven" (Divine Service Proper Preface) to feast upon the very Lamb of God. Yes, the Church is the land of the believers, the new Jerusalem, and the promised land, all wrapped up in the local congregation wherever "the Gospel is purely taught and the Sacraments are correctly administered" (Augsburg Confession VII 1–2).

God has taken the dry bones of all fallen sinners, and by His pastors He has preached a life-giving Gospel to them and brought them to the refreshing waters of the font. He has enlivened all who have passed through the holy font. And God is just as faithful has He was at the time of Ezekiel's vision. He will not lie. He calls His Church "a chosen race, a royal priesthood, a holy nation, a people for His own possession" and that is precisely what she is. She is the beloved bride of Jesus Christ, the ever-faithful Bridegroom. What joy it is for resurrected Christians to reside in the land called "the Church" where God feeds and nourishes His beloved unto life everlasting. Nothing comes closer to the vision of Ezekiel than this!

Conclusion

Ezekiel's vision of dry bones is truly one of a resurrection. The Lord's man speaks words of life and, just as in the rest of the Scriptures, things happen! Bones that are "very dry" are given flesh and the re-creating breath of the Spirit. This same thing happens at every baptismal font, where resurrections abound. Like the dry, dead bones, dead sinners are given the water of life as the Word of life is spoken in their ear: "I baptize you in the name of the Father, and of the Son, and of the Holy Spirit." Their dryness is met with the quenching tide of living water that flows from Jesus Himself (see John 4:7–15; 7:37–39; and

19:31–37) and by the creating breath of the Holy Spirit, they are re-created as newborn members of the body of Christ. Those once dry bones now stand as the faithful who are "coming out of the great tribulation. They have washed their robes and made them white in the blood of the Lamb" (Revelation 7:14).

Prayer

Come, you faithful, raise the strain
Of triumphant gladness!
God has brought His Israel
Into joy from sadness,
Loosed from Pharaoh's bitter yoke
Jacob's sons and daughters,
Led them with unmoistened foot
Through the Red Sea waters.

Alleluia! Now we cry To our King
immortal, Who, triumphant, burst
the bars
Of the tomb's dark portal.
Come, you faithful, raise the strain
Of triumphant gladness!
God has brought His Israel
Into joy from sadness!

("Come, You Faithful, Raise the Strain," *LSB* 487:1, *5; LW* 141:1, 5)

8
Ezekiel's Vision of Dry Bones

Introduction

Why is the vision of dry bones an odd choice for a reading on Pentecost Sunday? Read **Acts 2:1–36**. What is celebrated on Pentecost Sunday? Now read **John 6:63**, the explanation of the Third Article of the Apostles' Creed, and questions 157–161 from Luther's Small Catechism. What is the work of the Holy Spirit? After reading these, discuss whether or not **Ezekiel 37** is an appropriate reading for Pentecost Sunday.

The Lord's Man

Read **1 Timothy 4:14** and **2 Timothy 1:6**.
Pastors are ordained and put into the Lord's service through the laying on of hands. How did Ezekiel receive his own "laying on of hands"?

Read **Ezekiel 37**. The laying on of hands is a sacred act for a sacred task. What is that task for Ezekiel? He is given two "words" to speak (one binds and one loosens). What are those two words? How does he preach the Law?

Contrast **Ezekiel 7** with **Ezekiel 37**. Which one is a message of death and which is one of life? Is there a difference between the two in tone or intention?

Oh, the Places You'll Go!

Read **Luke 3:4–5**. What task is John the Baptizer given to do? How does Ezekiel's task prefigure that of John? How does a valley symbolize death, and why would it need to be raised up?

Compare the pastors of the Church with Ezekiel. How do they resemble this great prophet-priest? Think hands, spirit, task, words, and resurrection!

The Dryness of Death

Discuss the reasons why water is essential to life. Given the necessity of water, how do David's words in **Psalm 22** show Jesus to be the icon of dryness and death?

Imagine Jesus' looking at His fallen creation. How does what He would see compare to what Ezekiel does see in those "very dry" bones? Do either of them see life?

Is it realistic to think that dried-up bones, residing in a valley-grave, can ever come back to life?

Read **Revelation 7:9–17** and **Ezekiel 37:1–3**. Compare and contrast these two visions. How are they similar? How are they different?

Discuss a time when you were so awestruck that what was very apparent was still quite unbelievable. (E.g., A child turns sixteen years old, and his parents buy him a car for his birthday. However, when he first sees it, he is so overwhelmed that the parent says, "Do you know whose car this is?")

In the Lord's Stead

Read **Luke 10:17**. When a pastor speaks to his flock, whose voice is actually heard? Look at the Absolution in the Divine Service. In whose "stead" is the pastor standing and speaking and acting?

If Christ is the Word of God (**John 1:1**), and Ezekiel speaks that Word, then who do those dry bones hear?

Compare the cosmic nature of what ensues following Ezekiel's speaking and that which comes from Jesus' speaking at the cross on Good Friday.

New Creations

When the bones finally received sinews, flesh, and skin, were they complete? Read **Genesis 2:1–7**. What completes a person? What do these bones still need?

When the *ruach* is breathed into the newly created bodies, what will they become? Discuss how this is a return to the Garden of Eden, where the breath of God created Adam. When the Lord makes things new, how does He do it? Does He destroy what was and start over, or does He take what is there and re-create it?

Who Are These?

There is often an attempt among Christians to not look "weird" or "too Christian." But do the baptized look different than non-Christians? How so?

How is the "new look" for those former bones a picture of what happens to dead sinners who are baptized?

They Know the Lord

Many people think that they can know God through nature or by signs and wonders. Read **John 3:1–2**. Nicodemus does not get it right because he only knows Jesus as the wonder worker who is "a teacher come from God" (**v. 2**). This is not how the Lord would have you know Him, but how would He? Where does the Lord reveal who He really is and what His ultimate purpose is?

Discuss a time when you've been away from home. Why is it often very comforting to return home? Wouldn't you like a home you'd never have to leave?

The New House of Israel

Read **1 Peter 2:1–12**. Why is the message of St. Peter a fitting one for the newly baptized? Who is the new Israel? What have those newly baptized just entered into?

Since Israel and the Lord were as close as a husband and wife, discuss the idea that what happens to Israel will necessarily happen to Jesus and vice versa. Have you ever known of a spouse who suffers because the other spouse is suffering? Often, what happens to one to one spouse determines what will happen to the other. Why does the Church look like Christ? How do the people of the Church reflect the vision of dry bones? Who raised our dried-up, dead bodies to new life?

Dry Bones Given the Water of Life!

Why do some not see the Sacraments in the Gospel of John? How are their misunderstandings cleared up? Read **John 3:1–8**; **4:13–14**; **6:22–59**; and **19:31–37**. Now do you see them? The Sacraments are seen in the water, bread, and blood of John's Gospel.

By what means does the Holy Spirit convey the gift of life and resurrect our dead souls? When the Holy Spirit battles the demonic forces that reside in dead sinners, who is bound to win?

Creation was completed in seven days, but what happened to that creation? Why is the number eight a significant number?

Discuss what happens at the baptismal font. How does God use water to give His gift of new life and resurrection, and also quench the thirst of our dried-up souls?

The Dwelling Place of the Saints

The resurrected in **Ezekiel 37** were promised a home. Where is the home of those resurrected in the font?

3

Jonah

Lesson Focus

God sent Jonah to be the preacher for the Gentiles of Nineveh, but Jonah had other plans. After a nasty boat ride, crashing waves, and powerful winds, Jonah found himself in the belly of a great fish. There was no hope for life in that great fish, that is, unless God recalled Jonah from his watery grave to new life.

Gospel Focus

After three days in the deep, God brought the dead sinner Jonah out of the mouth of the great fish, alive and well again.

Prayer

O God, for our redemption You have given Your only-begotten Son to the death of the cross, and by His glorious resurrection You have delivered us from the power of our enemy. Therefore grant that all our sin may be drowned through daily repentance and that day by day a new man may arise to live before You in righteousness and purity forever; through Jesus Christ, Your Son, our Lord, who lives and reigns with You and the Holy Spirit, one God, now and forever. Amen. (Collect for the Resurrection of Our Lord, *LW*, p. 47)

Introduction

Jesus once told the seventy-two He was about to send out, "The harvest is plentiful, but the laborers are few. Therefore pray earnestly to the Lord of the harvest to send out laborers into His harvest" (Luke 10:2). But the need for laborers to work the harvest is really not a new thing. From as early as the fall into sin, God was dedicated to bringing all people out of a relationship with Adam and Eve and back into a relationship with Him. Whether it be to the slave-drivers from Egypt (Moses and Aaron) or the nasty people of Nineveh (Jonah), God needed preachers to proclaim the message of repentance and forgiveness of sins in the promised Messiah, Jesus Christ. Yet some, in their sin, refuse God's call and choose their own way. They separate themselves from God, and it is only by God's faithfulness to them that they are finally called from death in sin to new life in Him.

Reluctant Preacher

Can you imagine the worst job in the world? You would probably avoid that job at all costs, right? What if the Lord told you that's what he had in mind for you to do? How would you react to the Lord placing you in a vocation that you had no desire to fulfill?

Think about the quote from Chad Bird. Do you picture Jonah as a chicken, a hawk, or a vulture?

Have you ever thought about how willing God is to forgive you? Do you ever get frustrated with God's over-willingness to forgive?

If a man was called by God to serve a congregation as pastor, he would certainly not want to be called to the Ninevite congregation. The Ninevites were a group of violent Gentiles who fiercely opposed the Israelites (Jonah 3:8). Strangely enough, Jonah was an Israelite, the only prophet called by God to go to the Ninevites. Luther brings out the uniqueness of this calling by saying,

> *We do not read of another instance where God delegated a prophet to go so far away from the land of Israel and to such a mighty kingdom. Since this was an unusual and peculiar and unprecedented order, it puzzled and perplexed Jonah that God should select him from all others for this errand.* (AE 19:49)

Granted, the Ninevites needed a preacher. They needed someone to bring the message of God, in order that they might repent and turn from all their evil and wicked ways. But Jonah did not seem to think that he was the right guy for the job. He probably feared the Ninevites because they were Gentiles who were always looking to destroy God's chosen people, Israel. Moreover, if Jonah preached the message of repentance, and they did repent, he would be deemed a traitor, a helper of the enemy. In one of his sermons, Chad Bird describes Jonah this way:

> *Jonah's name means "dove," but he acted more like a chicken. That's our first impression anyhow. God points the dove-man toward Nineveh and he skedaddles to the seaside, finds his roost in a boat, and sets sail for the land called Tarshish. Jonah couldn't handle God's assignment. He chickened out. So it seems. But that's not really the problem. Jonah's no chicken; he's a hawk, or a vulture, or something in between, whatever bird wants a pound of Ninevite flesh. The only thing Jonah is afraid of is that God will be God. That's what irks him. The problem is not that he has bad theology, but that the good theology he knows rubs him the wrong way. He knows that God is good, gracious, loving, forgiving, and all those sorts of things. And he can't stand it. At least, if God is like that toward those undeserving, good-for-nothing Ninevites. Those dirtbags need to pay, burn, suffer. Come on, God, let's play the Sodom and Gomorrah card, and let 'em have it.* (*Christ Crucified: Lutheran Sermons* by Chad L. Bird [Grand Rapids, MI: Emmanuel Press, 2005], p. 36)

Declines the Call

Read Genesis 3. Imagine trying to hide from God in the Garden of Eden. Now read Jonah 1:3–4. Imagine being in Jonah's shoes and trying to flee from the Lord. Foolishness, right? Why is the natural reaction to a grave sin (in both cases, disobeying the command of the Lord) such foolishness? Can there ever be true comfort, relief, or joy in fleeing from the Lord?

Read Numbers 21:4–9. In what ways did the Israelites sin? The Lord's reaction to their sin was to allow the devil to run rampant amongst the children of God. Certainly the Lord causes no evil, but He may, for a time, allow it to happen. For what reason? God allowed the Israelites to experience evil in order that they could recognize their sin, repent, ask for forgiveness, and be healed. In what way did the Lord allow evil to happen to Jonah? For what reason?

The task was too great for the "dove man," and he ended up chickening out. Instead of going to Nineveh like God called him to do, he fled to Tarshish, the name of which means "a large sea which is not a lake" (AE 19:43). It is quite humorous that Jonah believed he could flee "away from the presence of the Lord" (Jonah 1:3). This is reminiscent of Adam and Eve who, after the fall, tried mightily to hide from the presence of the Lord among the trees in the Garden of Eden (Genesis 3:8). Can anyone really hide from God's presence? Absolutely not! Can anyone really flee to the sea to avoid God? Absolutely not! Yet, is this fleeing sin? Throughout the Early Church, there was much debate over whether or not Jonah's fleeing from the Lord was a sin. With Luther, there is no debate. It is a grave sin for Jonah to flee and decline the call of the Lord. Luther says of Jonah's attempt to flee from the Lord:

> *Thus we shall stick rigidly and inflexibly to the Word of God and agree that Jonah here committed a grave and serious sin. . . . Thus it is also evident that Jonah is disobedient to this earnest command of God by fleeing and refusing to execute God's command. Thereby he sinned as gravely as Adam did in Paradise. Jonah should not merely have accepted the divine will, but he should also have been most happy to carry it out. He should rather have suffered a hundred deaths than to become disobedient to God's Word. For what can be more flagrant and heinous than disobedience to God's will? Behold what a price Adam, Saul, and the people of Israel paid for this sin! Yes, witness what happened to Jonah here because of his disobedience!* (AE 19:45–46)

Jonah's unwillingness to heed the call of God should have meant certain death and eternal damnation. Those who transgress and deny God or His call do not deserve to live. Yet God is always patient with His children. Though they may leave Him, He will never leave them. This is especially the case with Jonah.

Instead of going to Nineveh, Jonah began to make his way to Joppa. And when he got there, he found a boat, paid the whole fare, and began his voyage as far away from the Lord as he could possibly get. But although he left the Lord behind him, the Lord never left him. It is very true that the Lord had every right to strike Jonah down immediately and cast him into the depths of hell for his disobedience. Yet God is always "slow to anger and abounding in steadfast love, and relenting from disaster" (Jonah 4:2). Out of mercy and love for Jonah, God did not punish Jonah as his sin deserved. He did, however, give the Law to Jonah in the form of a storm "The LORD hurled a great wind upon the sea, and there was a mighty tempest on the sea, so that the ship threatened to break up" (Jonah 1:4). In that great storm, God brought some to faith and drove others to repentance.

Sound Sleeper

Read Matthew 8:23–25. Now read Jonah 1:4–6. In what ways does Jonah resemble Jesus? Ultimately, who was it that could calm the storm on the great sea heading to Tarshish?

Read Jonah 1:7–16. How was it that the storm stopped its raging? Notice the connection once again between the death of Jonah and that of Jesus: both died for the life of man; those who hurl Jonah into the sea ask that their hands not be red with his innocent blood (like Pontius Pilate); in his death, others believed and they "feared the LORD exceedingly" (Jonah 1:16).

The great wind and mighty tempest that the Lord hurled upon the sea were so great that the boat carrying Jonah and the mariners was almost shattered to pieces. It is hard enough to imagine hurricane-force winds and large crashing waves, but it is even harder to imagine being in the midst of this storm with very little protection and safety. Yet this storm does not faze Jonah. He is probably exhausted from trying to flee from God and also filled with dread over his unwillingness to heed the call. The word used for his sleeping is *raw-dam*, giving the impression that this was not a regular catnap, but rather a deep, heavy sleep such as that caused by some traumatic event.

The mariners tried everything to stop this storm while Jonah slept below. They prayed to their gods and threw all the cargo overboard, but soon realized that nothing could halt this storm. Praying to foreign gods and a lighter ship could do nothing to bring the raging wind and sea under control. The only thing that could make this storm stop was the sound sleeper down below.

About eight hundred years after Jonah's ship experience, Jesus would have His own rough ride in a boat. Matthew says:

> *And when He got into the boat, His disciples followed Him. And behold, there arose a great storm on the sea, so that the boat was being swamped by the waves; but He was asleep. And they went and woke Him, saying, "Save us, Lord; we are perishing."* (8:23–25)

Both Jonah and Jesus were the key to calming their respective storms. Yet the plea to Jonah was not like the one to Jesus. The disciples implored Jesus to save them, whereas the mariners on the boat with Jonah implored him to "call out to your god!" (Jonah 1:6).

But interestingly enough, Jonah did not call out to his God. He just sat there, scared to death of what the Lord would do next and how these feisty mariners would react when they found out he was the source of all the evil. If they could just make it to dry land, all would be well. Yet, the fierce winds and waves did not show any sign of calming down. The mariners had to find out who or what was causing this great storm and make it stop, but no one was willing to confess. They were forced to cast lots.

The lot fell on Jonah. The one who frantically fled and soundly slept was now coerced into confession. All who were on the ship knew that he was responsible. Like an inquisition, they began a firing squad of questions. "What is your occupation? And where do you come from? What is your country? And of what people are you?" (Jonah 1:8). With that, Jonah was forced to 'fess up. The proverbial cat was out of the bag, and they knew he was the guilty party. "Jonah's confession is forthcoming; now the sin is brought to the light of day" (AE 19:63).

Jonah was the one responsible for all the evil that had ensued. He was a fearer of God, but he failed to follow His divine will. The only solution to the great storm was for Jonah to die. Once he was off that ship, all would be calm and well. Therefore, Jonah said to the other mariners, "Pick me up and hurl me into the sea; then the sea will quiet down for you, for I know it is because of me that this great tempest has come upon you" (Jonah 1:12). Jonah bore full responsibility and "renders satisfaction to love and makes amends to the people for subjecting them to danger" (AE 19:65). All are forgiven, and he alone would suffer.

So the mariners picked up the cause of the storm and threw him into the depths of the sea. The infection was officially out of the system. The rotten limb of the sailing body had officially been amputated. And with the sinner, Jonah, now drowning in the sea, the "sea ceased from its raging" (Jonah 1:15).

In Jonah's death, all others are forgiven. In Jonah's death, the raging storm ceases. In Jonah's death, the other men on the boat fear the Lord "exceedingly" (Jonah 1:16). In Jonah's death, the men on the boat believe and trust in the God of Abraham, Isaac, and Jacob. They trust in the God who would soon send His only Son into the world as a sacrifice for all sin. As Luther says, "for 'to fear God' is the Hebrew way of saying to worship God" (AE 19:64). In His death, others have faith!

Buried in the Great Fish

As Jonah sank to the bottom of the great sea, what did the mariners think his lot would be? Read verse 14 once again. Did the mariners think that Jonah had any chance of survival?

As Jonah was thrown overboard, he was essentially "as good as dead." The mariners believed he would die, and Jonah probably thought likewise. Moreover, Jonah was dead in his sin. He had fallen into the depths because of his rejections of God's command. Yet as he sank to his death, how did God come to his rescue?

The mariners believed that Jonah was dead. But as though drowning in a great sea was not bad enough, Jonah's problems appeared to become even worse. Not only were his lungs filling with water, and was it getting harder to swim, but now he went headlong into the belly of a great fish. This is the kind of stuff that one might find in an adventure book or great mystery. It is surreal to imagine that with one bite by the great fish, he could easily have lost a limb or his very life. Jonah was battling the waters and being eaten alive.

Although Jonah was certainly in desperate need, God promises never to leave or forsake His children. Jonah, though acting like a delinquent child, was one of God's own, and therefore, he would not be allowed to perish in his great travail.

To be sure, Jonah had hit the bottom of life. He was dead and buried in his sin and was lying in the depths (Latin Vulgate: *profundum*) of the earth. The depths of sin and shame is not a place where anyone would like to be. This is the place of St. Peter after his denial of Jesus Christ, and the place of all people after the fall into sin. In the depths, there is no place to turn but God. Just as a person who has flatlined in the emergency room cannot grab the paddles and bring themselves back to life, so also those who have fallen into sin like Jonah cannot bring themselves back to life unless God wills it and does it.

Even in sin and the depths of life, God never leaves a person, not even Jonah. God could have easily left Jonah to his sin and allowed the waters to consume him. But thankfully, He did not. Rather, even in Jonah's death to sin and ours, God is there, with His rich mercy and grace.

A Watery Grave

Some Early Church fathers believed that when Jonah cried out from the belly of "Sheol" (Jonah 2:2), he was actually crying out from the resting place of the dead saints. Although this may not be completely accurate, in what sense was Jonah dead?

Read Romans 6:3–4. In what way does the burial of Jonah in a watery grave prefigure us being "buried with Christ" in Holy Baptism? Read the Small Catechism on the Sacrament of Holy Baptism, part four. What is drowned and killed in the water of Holy Baptism? What emerges from the tomb of the font? How often should a person do the "Jonah thing," and be drowned, die, and emerge to new life?

Read Jonah 2:3–6. In the death of Jonah, the water does powerful things. How does the water of the baptismal font do powerful things?

People often use the term "the belly of the earth" to describe burial. This imagery comes from Jonah, who dies to his sin and is "buried" in the belly of the great fish. However, being in a belly presupposes that one will eventually come out, even if it is by vomiting, as in the case of Jonah. One would not say that a person is buried in "the belly of the earth" if they do not believe that one who is buried will eventually be "vomited" up out of the grave. To be a bit more refined, one does not speak of being buried in the "belly of the earth" unless they believe in the resurrection from that belly!

From the belly of the great fish, Jonah cries out to "the LORD his God" (Jonah 2:1) in psalm-like prayer. From the very beginning, Jonah acknowledges where he is and why he is there. He begins by saying that he called out to the Lord from his distress (Jonah 2:2), and that place of distress is the "belly of Sheol" (Jonah 2:2) or, as the NIV says, "from the depths of the grave." Either way, the emphasis is on Jonah being dead. In the Early Church, some thought that Sheol was the resting place of the dead saints of the Old Testament until the death and resurrection of Jesus Christ. It was not thought of as a place of torment or purging (i.e., purgatory), but simply as a place of resting and waiting for the resurrection of Jesus. Although this understanding of Sheol is not completely correct in the eyes of a Lutheran, the theological point the Early Church was trying to make was a good one. By Jonah saying that he was in Sheol, the place of resting for the dead, some concluded that he *actually died* in the belly of the great fish, and God, out of His infinite mercy, resurrected him from the dead.

Other great theologians, like Luther, have interpreted Sheol to mean hell, or a place of torment and distress. For Luther, though, this hell is the belly of the great fish:

> *When Jonah speaks of "the belly of Sheol," he means the belly of the fish. He calls it the belly of Sheol not because the fish is hell, but because the fish's belly was as dreadful as hell to him; Jonah experienced hell in it. He might have used the term "the belly of death" —not because the fish was the same as death, but because Jonah was suffering the agonies of death in it.* (AE 19:74)

Whether Jonah used Sheol to mean a resting place with the saints or a hellish place of torment, one must ask why he used such a term. Although Jonah probably did not physically die in the belly of that fish, he is, in essence, dead. He is well aware that his earthly life is nearly over, and as it was with Isaac on the three-day journey to Mount Moriah, Jonah knows that he is as good as dead. Moreover, he realizes that he is dead in sin. These two facts alone would have made his life a living "Sheol."

When sinners are left to deal with their sins on their own, their lives become like Jonah's—a "living hell." Luther uses these same words in the well-known hymn "Dear Christians, One and All, Rejoice" (*LSB* 556:2; *LW* 353:2).

Fast bound in Satan's chains I lay;
Death brooded darkly o'er me.
Sin was my torment night and day;
In sin my mother bore me.
But daily deeper still I fell;
My life became a living hell,
So firmly sin possessed me.

Yet it is only when a person has reached that bottomless pit and acknowledged that they cannot bring themselves out that they can receive the divine mercy of God. Luther brilliantly gave words to this hellish state of being when he wrote:

From depths of woe I cry to Thee,
In trial and tribulation;
Bend down Thy gracious ear to me,
Lord hear my supplication.
If Thou rememb'rest ev'ry sin,
Who then could heaven ever win
Or stand before Thy presence?
("From Depths of Woe I Cry to Thee," *LSB* 607:1; *TLH* 329:1)

By nature, all human beings are in the depths of woe, even from the time they are conceived in their mother's womb (Psalm 51:5). All people are dead or, in the original Greek, *nekros* in their trespasses and sins (Ephesians 2:1). None of us, of our own nature, has any life in us, but we are rather like rotten, smelly roadkill. The Lutheran Confessions clearly explain this sinful nature:

Our churches teach that since the fall of Adam [Romans 5:12], all who are naturally born are born with sin [Psalm 51:5], that is, without the fear of God, without trust in God, and with the inclination to sin, called concupiscence.
Concupiscence is a disease and original vice that is truly sin. It damns and brings eternal death on those who are not born anew through Baptism and the Holy Spirit [John 3:5]. (AC II 1–2)

Human beings are conceived and born in the depths of sin and death, and all they deserve is eternal damnation. However, as shown in the account of Jonah, God loves to deliver people from the depths of sinful woe by means of raging water. "And the flood surrounded me; all your waves and your billows passed over me" (Jonah 2:3).

In the story of Jonah, water has the power to do amazing, even deadly, things. Water can easily kill and, as Jonah said, it certainly tried to destroy him (Jonah 2:5). Yet it is this same water that brings life and deliverance. The Lord is in total control of His creation, so He can use this same deadly water to bring life and immortality to light.

These words of Jonah are also the words of every baptized Christian. Even in the depths of sin and death, children, young and old, are surrounded by a great flood, with waves and billows passing over as they make their way through the font of Holy Baptism. Just as Jonah "died" in the great fish, so do all people die to sin and rise in new life (Romans 6:3–4) as they make their way through the belly of the baptismal font. In essence, Jonah received a type of Baptism. He was in the belly of the great fish for one reason: his sin. Because of his sin, he was destined for death, and was already as good as dead. Yet, even as the waves billowed over him (Jonah 2:3) and waters threatened to take his life (Jonah 2:5), God was merciful and brought Jonah's life up from the pit of his sin and death (Jonah 2:6). In other words, Christ resurrected Jonah from his death in sin, and through water Christ brought Jonah up in newness of life.

Resurrection from a Belly

Read Matthew 12:40. Jesus said that the Scriptures bear witness about Him (see John 5:39). The Scriptures He is referring to are not the Gospels or Epistles. Rather, the Scriptures are the Old Testament. In what way is Jonah's death, burial, and resurrection a prefiguring of the death, burial, and resurrection of Christ?

Compare the ways in which the cosmos is

altered in both the death of Jonah and that of Jesus.

Although Jonah did not always get everything right (e.g., denied God's call, fled from His presence, etc.), by the end of his three days in the great fish, Jonah clearly and concisely stated the key to all orthodox Christian theology, "Salvation belongs to the LORD!" (Jonah 2:9). Jonah got it! He knew full well that in the belly of that great fish there was death that resulted from his own actions. However, he knew that life and salvation is solely a gift from the Lord's love.

Jonah's death, rest (burial) in the watery grave, and resurrection from the belly of the great fish prefigures the death, burial, and resurrection of Jesus Christ. Jesus Himself says, "For just as Jonah was three days and three nights in the belly of the great fish, so will the Son of Man be three days and three nights in the heart of the earth" (Matthew 12:40). It all took place on a miserable Friday afternoon. There, on the place of the skull, the Lord Jesus Christ died in the place of all sinners as He willingly hung on the cross as the chief sinner.

This, however, is not an ordinary death, because this is not an ordinary sinner. Rather, this is God in the flesh, bearing the sins of the whole world. As Luther says: "And all the prophets saw this, that Christ was to become the greatest thief, murderer, adulterer, robber, desecrater, blasphemer, etc., there has ever been anywhere in the world" (AE 26:277). Yes, all the prophets did see this, even Jonah, who saw it in his own suffering, death, and resurrection from the great fish.

Jesus Christ bears the sins of the world in an event that is unmatched in history. This cataclysmic event, where God in the flesh suffers and dies for all sinners, is an event that rocks the cosmos. When the God-man, Jesus Christ, dies, skies are darkened, graves open up, the temple curtain is torn asunder, and a world riddled with sin is released from its bondage. And Jonah himself, in undergoing his own quasi-cataclysmic event, prefigures Jesus Christ.

Jonah "died" in the great fish, as floods surrounded him, waves billowed over him (Jonah 2:3), waters closed in to take his life, weeds enveloped his head, and bars locked him in (Jonah 2:5–6). In Jonah's "death," the cosmos did strange things. No one would ever imagine simple water doing such great and powerful things. Yet, in Christ's death, the cosmos does not merely do strange things, but is forever changed.

The cosmos, which came into being through God's creating Word over seven days, is re-created with Jesus' death and subsequent resurrection. It is no mistake that Christ rises from the dead, completing His act of creating all things new, on the eighth day. Seven is the number of completion, but eight is the number of new creation. Jesus Christ rises from the dead on the day of the new creation because, in His salvific act (suffering, death, and resurrection), Christ makes all things new, even Jonah. Sinful creation and sinful human beings are re-created and stand before God in newness of life.

Resurrection from the Belly of the Font

In the account of Jonah and the great fish, it is the Lord who spoke to the waters. In what way does the Lord still speak to water to do such amazing things as kill and give life?

How does the death, burial, and resurrection of Jesus stand at the center of all history? In what way are all resurrections a picture of His own glorious resurrection?

God uses life-threatening water to bring Jonah to new life as He resurrects ("vomits" [Jonah 2:10]) Jonah from the belly of the great fish. In the same way, God uses life-threatening, raging water to drown the sins of all who pass through the belly of the baptismal font. Like Jonah, all sinners who pass through that life-giving belly come out whole, forgiven, and newly created. However, there is no resurrection unless there is a death.

In the words of Dr. Norman Nagel, "Water

does to death and brings to life" (*Lutheran Worship: History and Practice*, p. 264). How can water do such amazing things as kill and resurrect? Just as they did those things to Jonah! With the command and Word of God, water has the power to kill a person and, at the same moment, bring them to life. "The LORD spoke to the fish" (Jonah 2:10) just as He speaks at every font. He says, "I baptize you in the name of the Father, and of the + Son, and of the Holy Spirit" (*LSB*, p. 270; *LW*, p. 202). But the Lord could not speak to the fish and He could not speak at the font if it were not for Jesus and His death, burial, and resurrection.

Jesus makes all things new when He completes the act of salvation on the eighth day by rising from the grave. That eighth day stands at the center of all history. Everything that came before and everything that would come after finds its origin and meaning in this day of the new creation. Jonah's resurrection happens because Christ would be resurrected. The resurrection from sin in the font happens because Christ has been resurrected. The great baptismal hymn gets it right when it proclaims:

We know that Christ is raised and dies
no more.
Embraced by death, He broke its fearful
hold;
And our despair He turned to blazing joy.
Alleluia!

We share by water in His saving death.
Reborn, we share with Him an Easter life
As living members of a living Christ.
Alleluia!

The Father's splendor clothes the Son
with life.
The Spirit's power shakes the Church
of God.
Baptized, we live with God the Three
in One.
Alleluia!

("We Know That Christ Is Raised,"
© John B. Geyer, *LSB* 603; *HS98* 846)

Conclusion

How have you been vomited up from a belly like Jonah?

Once damned sinners pass through the belly of the font and are "vomited" up on the other side, they share with Jesus—and Jonah—in an "eighth day" Easter life. They are made new. Although they were once dead, they are now alive. They are new creations, both in the sight of God and of men. As newly resurrected creations, they bear witness to the hope that they have because of the mercy of God. Jonah's resurrection leads him to preach as the Lord asked him to do. He will sacrifice and do as he has vowed (Jonah 2:9). This is his heartfelt "Amen" to the gracious gift of God. In a similar way, baptismal resurrection leads the Christian to pay what they have vowed, or in other words, "to confess, to praise, and to proclaim the Lord and thus to honor and to serve Him" (AE 19:82).

What Luther said of Jonah can be said of all baptized Christians: "Death and sin are an opportunity for life and righteousness" (AE 19:21). Life and righteousness come because of God's mercy in sending His Son to suffer, die, be buried, and rise again on the day of the new creation, so that all the sinful, dead "Jonahs" of this world would have new life.

Prayer

O God, as the prophet Jonah spent three days in the belly of the great fish, so Your Son Jesus spent three days in the heart of the earth. Grant us repentance to embrace our death in Him through Holy Baptism and to proclaim His victory over sin and death to all the world; through the same Jesus Christ, our Lord.
(Collect for the Easter Vigil, *LSB Lectionary: Series C,* p. 187).

3

JONAH

Reluctant Preacher

Can you imagine the worst job in the world? You would probably avoid that job at all costs, right? What if the Lord told you that's what He had in mind for you to do? How would you react to the Lord placing you in a vocation you had no desire to fulfill?

Think about the quote from Chad Bird. Do you picture Jonah as a chicken, a hawk, or a vulture?

Have you ever thought about how willing God is to forgive you? Do you ever get frustrated with God's over-willingness to forgive?

Declines the Call

Read **Genesis 3**. Imagine trying to hide from God in the Garden of Eden. Now read **Jonah 1:3–4**. Imagine being in Jonah's shoes and trying to flee from the Lord. Foolishness, right? Why is the natural reaction to a grave sin (in both cases, disobeying the command of the Lord) such foolishness? Can there ever be true comfort, relief, or joy in fleeing from the Lord?

Read **Numbers 21:4–9**. In what ways did the Israelites sin? The Lord's reaction to their sin was to allow the devil to run rampant amongst the children of God. Certainly the Lord causes no evil, but He may, for a time, allow it to happen. For what reason? God allowed the Israelites to experience evil in order that they could recognize their sin, repent, ask for forgiveness, and be healed. In what way did the Lord allow evil to happen to Jonah? For what reason?

Sound Sleeper

Read **Matthew 8:23–25**. Now read **Jonah 1:4–6**. In what ways does Jonah resemble Jesus? Ultimately, who was it that could calm the storm on the great sea heading to Tarshish?

Read **Jonah 1:7–16**. How was it that the storm stopped its raging? Notice the connection once again between the death of Jonah and that of Jesus: both died to save the lives of men; those who hurl Jonah into the sea ask that their hands not be red with his innocent blood (like Pontius Pilate); in his death, others believed and they "feared the Lord exceedingly" (**Jonah 1:16**).

Buried in the Great Fish

As Jonah sank to the bottom of the great sea, what did the mariners think his lot would be? Read **verse 14** once again. Did the mariners think that Jonah had any chance of survival?
As Jonah was thrown overboard, he was essentially "as good as dead." The mariners believed he would die, and

Jonah probably thought likewise. Moreover, Jonah was dead in his sin. He had fallen into the depths because of his rejections of God's command. Yet as he sank to his death, how did God come to his rescue?

A Watery Grave

Some Early Church fathers believed that when Jonah cried out from the belly of "Sheol" (**Jonah 2:2**), he was actually crying out from the resting place of the dead saints. Although this may not be completely accurate, in what sense was Jonah dead?

Read **Romans 6:3–4**. In what way does the burial of Jonah in a watery grave prefigure us being "buried with Christ" in Holy Baptism? Read the Small Catechism on the Sacrament of Holy Baptism, part four. What is drowned and killed in the water of Holy Baptism? What emerges from the tomb of the font? How often should a person do the "Jonah thing," and be drowned, die, and emerge to new life?

Read **Jonah 2:3–6**. In the death of Jonah, the water does powerful things. How does the water of the baptismal font do powerful things?

Resurrection from a Belly

Read **Matthew 12:40**. Jesus said that the Scriptures bear witness about Him (see **John 5:39**). The Scriptures He is referring to are not the Gospels or Epistles. Rather, the Scriptures are the Old Testament. In what way is Jonah's death, burial, and resurrection a prefiguring of the death, burial, and resurrection of Christ?

Compare the ways in which the cosmos is altered in both the death of Jonah and that of Jesus.

Resurrection from the Belly of the Font

In the account of Jonah and the great fish, it is the Lord who spoke to the waters. In what way does the Lord still speak to water to do such amazing things as kill and give life?

How does the death, burial, and resurrection of Jesus stand at the center of all history? In what way are all resurrections a picture of His own glorious resurrection?

Conclusion

How have you been vomited up from a belly like Jonah?

4

Widow's Son at Nain

Lesson Focus

Throughout the Holy Scriptures, and especially the Gospels, death and life collide head-on. Thankfully, where Jesus is, there is life, and in the end, life always rules the day. In this lesson, Jesus Christ, who bears in His body life and immortality, comes head-to-head with a son who bears in his body death.

Prayer

Praise the Almighty, my soul, adore Him!
Yes, I will laud Him until death;
With songs and anthems I come before Him
As long as He allows me breath.
From Him my life and all things came;
Bless, O my soul, His holy name.
Alleluia, alleluia!
("Praise the Almighty,"
LSB 797:1; *LW* 445:1)

Introduction

Throughout Jesus' earthly ministry, He is always doing four things: (1) moving, (2) having compassion, (3) touching, and (4) healing. Jesus says things like, "Let us go on to the next towns" (Mark 1:38), and when He gets there He has compassion, stretches forth His hand, gives His touch, and grants healing to the sick, dying, or dead. This account of the widow's son at Nain is no different. Jesus, life incarnate, meets death head-on, but with His holy touch Christ brings life and immortality.

Death and Taxes

We live in a day and age when people are trying to avoid death at all cost. Why do you think people want to avoid dying? Have you ever heard that death is "natural" and just a part of life?

Read Genesis 1 and 2. In the creation account, is there any talk of death? Is death really "natural"? Yet if people believe that death is "natural" why do they try to avoid it so much? Is there any

chance death may not be "natural" but rather a result of sin and a consequence of living in a fallen world?

Death is certainly not foreign to us. It has been said that a person can count on two things: death and taxes! For us, death is sure, but how about for God?

People are always trying to avoid death. Some eat certain foods. Others live in certain areas. Some even have themselves frozen in hopes that they can be thawed and live again. Yet this world is not ruled by life, but by death. People die every day because death has dominion over creation and has ever since the time of Adam and Eve. Try as they may, no one can escape death's tight grip. Funeral homes will never go out of business because humans are dust, and to dust they shall return (Genesis 3:19).

Although the way of death is the way things are bound to go, it is not natural, and it was never intended to rule over creation. Therefore, no person should ever die, but, because of sin, all people will. However, death belongs to human beings and not to God. For this reason, the things of God are utterly opposed to death.

On the Road Again

Read Luke 7:11–17. In all of Jesus' moving about, where is His ultimate destination? (See Luke 9:51.) What's in Jerusalem that makes it the holy city? Now read John 2:18–22. What is going to happen to that temple?

Read Genesis 22:1–8. Recall the three-day journey of Isaac to his death on Mount Moriah (the land where Jerusalem would one day be built). How is Isaac's journey a microcosm of Jesus' three-year journey to the cross in Jerusalem?

The widow's son is dead and therefore completely defiled. Jesus is completely holy (see Acts 4:27 and the reference to "holy servant Jesus") as He is God in the flesh. Why would the God-man, who is completely holy, even come near to that which is unholy and defiled?

How is Jesus' whole life really a confrontation between life and death? Jesus became man at the incarnation for what reason?

What is the status of the woman whom Jesus meets? She is not only lonely because her son is dead, but she is now an outcast. Why? How is Jesus' stopping to help the widow a picture of what He came to this earth to do?

Not long after Jesus heals the centurion's servant, He is on the move once again. This time, Jesus is off to the town called Nain, from which He will definitely move again. Eventually, He will come to Jerusalem, the holy city, the place of His death. It is as though Jesus has a one-way ticket to His death, and all these stops are just pictures or moments of insight into what is to come. Even here, at Nain, Jesus gives a glimpse of what will come to fullness in Jerusalem at the cross. It must never be forgotten that His ultimate destination is that holy city.

Just two chapters later, Jesus will "set His face to go to Jerusalem" (Luke 9:51), but for now He is passing through the city called Nain. As Jesus makes His way into the city gate, a strange thing happens: He is confronted by a procession. This is not just any procession; it is a procession of people carrying a dead young man. Jesus Christ, who has resurrection and life in His very being (John 11:25), confronts a young man who bears only the marks of death. Moreover, the death of this man has left a mother with no one. The woman is already a widow (Luke 7:12) and now her son is gone as well. Imagine this scene as life meets death, and they clash like two soldiers on the battlefield.

This is not only the story of this text, but the whole story of the incarnation, in which God took on flesh and became man in Jesus Christ. Since the fall into sin, this world has only known sin and death. Yet, in the incarnation, life and immortality itself, God in the flesh, came into our world and invaded our creation. Life meets death head-on in the incarnation, when Jesus enters the womb of the Virgin Mary because, ultimately, that life has one purpose: to destroy death forever! The incarnation is nothing short of a cosmic event, and it remains unmatched until the crucifixion, where life defeats death forever. That is, of course, why Jesus came in the flesh and why He meets the widow's son at the gate in this text, "to re-create His fallen creatures" (*Luke 1:1–9:50* by Arthur A. Just Jr., p. 307) and to replace death with life.

Lacking a son and a husband, this widow is reduced to being a nobody. She will likely be overlooked in the days ahead by everyone she meets, that is, everyone except Jesus. Jesus journeys to her city, meets the funeral procession, and immediately shows concern for her well-being. Notice, Jesus does not stop for anyone else, not even for the large crowd coming toward Him. Rather, His attention is on the grieving mother. He stops only for her. Jesus sees that she is in a state of utter desperation since death has destroyed all that she loves. For this reason, Jesus is about to put true light back into her dark world and life back into her dead, only-begotten son.

True Compassion

Have you ever experienced the death of a loved one or a loved one of a close friend? Discuss how awkward this type of situation can be, especially when it comes to finding the right words to say.

As members of the body of Christ, it is our duty and privilege to show compassion, since our way is the "Jesus way." Yet this is not always easy, and, frankly, it is impossible. Why?

It is a heresy to say that God is, of His essence, wrathful. Rather, He is loving, compassionate, and so forth. With that said, how is Jesus' compassion different from ours?

For many people, one of the most awkward moments is shortly after a death. It is hard to find the right words at what seems to be one of the most difficult times. One would imagine that if death was as "natural" as the world makes it out to be, people would know precisely what to say! Yet often people end up offering words of consolation to the bereaved in ways that are not consoling at all. Things like, "He was a good man" or "You can always have more children" are of no comfort when a person is grieving the loss of a loved one. This lack of tact, though, really flows from a lack of true compassion. If a person's heart does not truly go out to the bereaved, and they do not experience all the pain of the one who has just lost a loved one, they will probably not be able to speak true words of compassion, comfort, and consolation.

Imagine what would have happened if Jesus would have consoled the grieving mother with, "Your son was a good man." It would not be long before someone in the crowd, or even the mother herself, would have lashed out at Jesus for His trite remark. But Jesus does not console with empty words that lack true compassion. As He sees the grieving mother, Jesus says to her, "Do not weep" (Luke 7:13). Do not weep? What does He expect? A widow has just lost her only son and only hope of actually having a place in this world, and Jesus is telling her not to cry. Outrageous!

True, it does seem a bit outrageous, but one must also remember why Jesus is saying this. Why does He tell her not to weep? Because, the text says, "He had compassion on her" (Luke 7:13). Jesus tells the mother not to weep because of His compassion. This, however, is not a halfhearted condolence or false empathy on Jesus' part, but true compassion. This word for compassion "is a graphic one that if taken literally would mean the complete outpouring of the inward parts" (Just, p. 308). Jesus has compassion from His insides, or His bowels. This is the deepest compassion a person can ever have, but it is only possible with the incarnate Son of God. Only He is, by His very essence, love and compassion.

Because Jesus has compassion from the very depths of His being, He is about to give the grieving mother a reason not to weep, for "'compassion' denotes an outpouring of mercy" (Just, p. 308). In the early twentieth century, the Lutheran theologian Dr. Paul E. Kretzmann wrote in his *Popular Commentary of the Bible*:

> *When Jesus saw the funeral procession and noticed the peculiar sadness of the burial, His heart was moved with the deepest sympathy for the bereaved mother. . . . His word to the widow was: "Weep not!" With what an expression of heartfelt compassion Jesus must have spoken the word, and how fully the poor woman realized the cordiality of the greeting and its power, to which she clung!* (*New Testament,* vol. 1, p. 302)

Jesus, the compassionate one, has compassion on the woman out of divine love and mercy, but also because of the special care He shows toward "the widows and the fatherless" (Psalm 146: 9). In this single account, Jesus brings the words of the psalmist to fruition as He has compassion on a widow and her fatherless son.

A Compassionate Touch

Think of a time when you really just needed a hug, a pat on the back, or a kind handshake. Have you ever noticed how the touch of a loved one can be comforting in a time of distress? Why do you think Jesus does not touch the widow? In what way does He actually extend His touch to her?

When Jesus touches the bier, is there any chance He will become unclean? How is His touch of the bier actually a picture of the cross?

Read stanza 2 of "The Infant Priest Was Holy Born" (*LSB* 624; *HS98* 853). What is it that "brings sanctity" or holiness to the unholy and defiled?

Read the Augsburg Confession, Article II. How has Jesus stopped our own burial processions?

Jesus shows true compassion from His insides to the woman but, ironically, His touch is given to someone else. It is not hard to imagine how nice it would have been for Jesus to put His arms around that grieving mother and give her a loving embrace. Yet instead of touching the grieving mother who is in need of comfort and compassion, Jesus touches death itself.

Today, this does not appear to be a big deal. People who grieve often want to have one last touch before the casket is closed or lowered into the ground. Moreover, there are often pallbearers who hold and touch the casket as it is carried from the church or funeral home out to the grave. In today's culture, people are accustomed to touching things saturated with death, like caskets or the deceased. However, this was unheard of at the time of Jesus. For Jesus to touch a bier like He does in this text would have not only been outrageous, but it should have rendered Him unclean. Jesus would have done better to give His touch to the mother, rather than to her son. However, Jesus came to bring life, and His touch will do just that, which, in turn, will bring comfort and peace to the grieving mother. Jesus is really embracing the grieving mother through the touch of her dead son!

The uncleanness that is rendered when one touches a bier (casket) comes from Levitical law in the Old Testament. In Leviticus 21, the Lord gave this charge to Moses and the other priests: "No one shall make himself unclean for the dead among his people, except for his closest relatives, his mother, his father, his son, his daughter, his brother, or his virgin sister (who is near to him because she has had no husband; for her he may make himself unclean)" (vv. 1–3). It was considered unclean to touch a dead person or the thing they were being carried on (bier). Yes, special exceptions were given to blood relatives, but that did not prevent the uncleanliness that came along with such an act.

Why could a priest not touch a corpse? The priest was God's representative on earth. What happened to him essentially happened to God. If the priest was defiled, then God was defiled. This is because God is holy and clean while a corpse is common and unclean. The common and unclean has no place within the realm of God, the holy and clean. Using Leviticus 10:10, the Rev. Dr. John Kleinig, in his commentary on the Book of Leviticus, provides an excellent exposition on the categories of holiness and cleanliness. He says:

> *The pole opposite to holiness was the state of impurity. It was completely incompatible with God's holiness, just as darkness and death are incompatible with light and life. Like holiness, impurity was both a power and a state of being. It too was never defined in abstract terms, but was associated with those unnamed, destructive forces that were opposed to God: powers that were unleashed by the transgression of His prohibitions, such as disorder, sin, sickness, death, and the spirits of the underworld.* (*Leviticus,* p. 8)

Jesus Christ, the great High Priest, is the holiness of God in the flesh. The corpse of the dead man lying on the bier is one of the most impure things imaginable. Jesus, holiness and purity incarnate, touches the casket of the dead man and risks being unclean in the sight of God. This touch is nothing less than a picture of the cross. There, at the cross, the holy, pure, undefiled God-man actually bears the sins of the entire world, and renders Himself unclean in the eyes of the Father and is forsaken for that reason. However, Jesus Christ cannot be overcome by the unclean, unholy things of this world because He created this world and has all power over it. The hymn "The Infant Priest Was Holy Born" says:

> *This great High Priest in human flesh*
> *Was icon of God's righteousness.*
> *His hallowed touch brought sanctity;*
> *His hand removed impurity.*
> (*LSB* 624:2; *HS98* 853:2)

Death is completely impure and unholy. Yet the hand of the God-man, Jesus Christ, has the power to make even a corpse holy and pure. How does He make this dead man holy and pure? He raises him from the dead. "The power of holiness and of life is in him. He brings purity to the unclean situation, not vice versa" (*Just*, p. 308). Jesus has only life, love, and mercy to give, and He gives it all to the widow's son at Nain. He touches the bier holding the dead young man and speaks those life-giving words, "Young man, I say to you, arise" (Luke 7:14). The word that Jesus uses for "arise" is *egerthetee*. This is no coincidence, since this is the word often used to speak of Jesus' resurrection from the grave. The young man is not simply told to "arise," but he is told to "resurrect" from the dead. As Kretzmann says:

> *The hand of Life rapped at the chamber of death. Those who carried the coffin stood at the touch of the Lord's hand. Then Jesus, as the Lord of life and death, gave a peremptory command: Young man, to thee I say, arise! He speaks to the dead as though he were merely sleeping. (Kretzmann,* p. 302*)*

In this text, Jesus not only moves into action, but with His touch and word, He shows why He comes into this world. He does not come to sympathize with to the widow over her loss. Nor does Jesus make an attempt to avoid the procession so that they might go to bury the dead young man. Rather, He heads off death itself; as He touches the bier, the procession of death comes to a screeching halt. God has come to bring salvation. He has come to make right that which has gone terribly wrong. It is not right that people die. Death is not natural. Rather, it is right that people have life and have it in abundance (John 10:10). And that is what Jesus has come to bring—life.

It's All in the Word

Listen to the quote from the writings of Martin Luther. Was Jesus active and working at creation? In what way? How does that Word still speak to this day?

Read the following:

Genesis 1:1–3

Psalm 29

Mark 1:40–45

John 11:38–44

Matthew 26:26–29

What happens when the Lord speaks? Does He speak realities, that is, do things do what He tells them to do? What does He say to the widow's son at Nain? What is the result of that Word?

John writes in his Gospel, "In the beginning was the Word, and the Word was with God, and the Word was God (1:1) . . . In Him was life, and the life was the light of men (1:4). . . And the Word became flesh and dwelt among us" (1:14). The Word of God, Jesus Christ, is from the beginning. Compare the beginning of Genesis with that of John: "In the beginning . . ." This is no coincidence. God creates things with His Word. As Genesis 1:3 states, "And God said. . ." When God speaks, things happen, and when God speaks at creation, the Word that He speaks is none other the Word which John describes, the Word made flesh.

Read this quote from Luther to your students:

> *Now compare with this [Genesis 1:3] the Gospel of John (1:1): "In the beginning was the Word." He is in proper agreement with Moses. He says: "Before the creation of the world there was not a single one of the creatures, but God nevertheless had the Word." What is this Word, or what did He do? Listen to Moses. The light, he says, was not yet in existence; but out of its state of being nothing the darkness was turned into that most outstanding creature, light. Through what? Through the Word. Therefore in the beginning and before every creature there is the Word, and it is such a power-*

> *ful Word that it makes all things out of nothing. From this follows without possibility of contradiction what John expressly adds: "This Word is God and yet is a Person distinct from God the Father, just as a word and he who utters a word are separate entities." Yet this distinction is such that, to use the expression, a most single singleness of essence remains.* (AE 1:16–17)

Jesus is the Word spoken at creation, for what is given to one divine person of the Holy Trinity to do is given to all the persons to do. Jesus Christ is just as integral a part in creation as the Father who speaks and the Holy Spirit who "was hovering over the face of the waters" (Genesis 1:2). Jesus is the Word who creates at creation and is continually re-creating through His voice, both spoken and attached to concrete things like water, bread, and wine.

With this, it is clear that every time the Lord's voice is heard in the Scriptures and something subsequently happens, this voice is none other than the voice of Jesus, communicating through whatever means He has chosen to use. When Jesus, the Word, speaks, it always happens, because Jesus, the Word, always speaks realities.

Here are a few examples: In Genesis 1:3, God speaks, "Let there be light," and what happens? There is light. In Psalm 29:3, "the voice of the LORD is over the waters"; it "breaks the cedars" (v.5); "flashes forth flames of fire" (v. 7); "shakes the wilderness" (v. 8); "makes the deer give birth and strips the forests bare" (v. 9). In Mark 1:41, the voice of that Word made flesh says to the leper "be clean" and what happens? He is clean. In John 11:43, Jesus says to dead Lazarus "come out" and what happens? He does. And in the Upper Room on Maundy Thursday, Jesus speaks to bread and wine saying, "This is My body . . . this is My blood" (Matthew 26:26, 28) and it is! When Jesus, the Word, speaks, it always happens.

There can therefore be no doubt that when the Word speaks, "Young man, I say to you, arise," the dead son will certainly do as the all-creating and redeeming Word has said. And so he does! The young man is resurrected from that unclean mat of death and granted new life by the Word of life, Jesus Christ. What at a joy it is to know that when He speaks, things happen!

Moving to the Font

If you had to describe our sinful condition, what words would you use? Given what you know about the disease of sin, how do you compare to the widow's son at Nain? How are you dead?

If you are dead, is there any chance that you can bring yourself back to life? Since bringing yourself back is an utter impossibility, who has to do it for you? How does He do it?

Read Luther's Small Catechism on Holy Baptism, part two. How is Jesus' resurrection of the widow's son at Nain a picture of what happens at every baptismal font? Who is it that meets you at the font?

Article II of the Augsburg Confession on Original Sin states, "Our churches teach that since the fall of Adam [Romans 5:12], all who are naturally born are born with sin [Psalm 51:5], that is, without the fear of God, without trust in God, and with the inclination to sin, called concupiscence" (AC II 1–2). However, this "Concupiscence" is not merely an inclination to sin, but it "is a disease and original vice that is truly sin" (AC II 2). What is the lot of those affected by this disease? "It damns and brings eternal death on those who are not born anew through Baptism and the Holy Spirit [John 3:5]" (AC II 2). Before Baptism, all human beings are spiritually dead (Ephesians 2:1). Although a person may live a long life on this earth, without Baptism his soul is no different than the body of that man on the bier being carried to his grave.

All human beings are children of Adam and Eve. Like children who inherit many physical traits from their earthly parents, all people have inherited sin from Adam and Eve. This sin is mortal sin, and it will eventually lead to death. For this reason, the children of Adam and Eve are in a great state of need, the need for life and salvation. Like the young man in this text, all people are in need of the compassionate touch of the great physician, Jesus Christ. Only he can bring their dead souls and dying bodies back to true life. The widow's son at Nain is a picture of what happens at every baptismal font. In the words of the Small Catechism, the answer to the question "What benefits does Baptism give?" is, "It works forgiveness of sins, rescues from death and the devil, and gives eternal salvation to all who believe this, as the words and promises of God declare" (Holy Baptism, Second Part).

No sinful, dead person can bring themselves to Jesus for this healing. Rather, Jesus comes to them. He moves to every font where His name (Father, Son, and Holy Spirit) is invoked and connected to water. Just as He goes from village to village doing what He has been sent to do, so does He go from Christian font to Christian font, doing what He loves to do—give life!

Compassion and Touch at the Font

Jesus meets dead sinners at the font to baptize them and give them life. For what reason does He do this? How is Jesus' yearning for you even deeper than that of a mother yearning for her child?

Examine the service of Holy Baptism (*LSB*, p. 268; *LW*, p. 199). In what ways does the pastor resemble Jesus Christ in this account of the widow's son at Nain? Any moving? Any speaking? Any touching? Any language of "new life"?

Listen to Gerhard's "Thanksgiving for Conversion" prayer. Often people have trouble admitting that they are spiritually dead and unable to bring themselves back to life. Why is this so? Is it hard to give the glory and honor to someone else? Yet in the act of salvation or conversion, who always does the verbs? Who brings life and resurrection to dead sinners at the font?

When Christ arrives at the font, He always has compassion. As it goes with the widow's son at Nain, so it goes with all dead sinners who approach the font for new life. As we read earlier, Jesus' unique compassion comes from the innermost part of His being, from His insides. In the account of the widow's son, Jesus shows this unique compassion to a mother who has lost the son who came from her own womb. In a unique event that is anything but coincidence, Jesus yearns and His insides go out to the one who has just lost the fruit of her insides. Although Jesus is not a mother, He certainly has a relationship with those He loves that is "deeper than child in the womb" (*Selected Sermons of Norman Nagel: From Valparaiso to St. Louis*, p. 92). Jesus yearns like a mother from His insides, just as the mother yearns for the one who came forth from her insides. Where there is compassion, a touch will quickly follow.

There is a story of a little boy who after a church service saw his pastor in his vestments and greeted him at the door by saying, "Hello, Jesus." One might ask if this is a proper greeting for a pastor. Well, yes and no. With regard to the latter, the pastor is certainly not Jesus. He is a sinner just like everyone else in the church. Yet, with regard to the former, he does stand in the place of Jesus when he gives the Lord's gifts with his hands and his mouth. When speaking of the ministry of the apostles, which has been passed on through the laying on of hands to the pastors of this day, St. Paul writes, "This is how one should regard us, as servants of Christ and stewards of the mysteries of God" (1 Corinthians 4:1). This young boy thought that the pastor was Jesus! Why? He thought he was Jesus because the pastor, as the steward of the mysteries of God (Sacraments), had baptized him. At the font, the pastor had touched the boy's forehead and heart, and poured water on him, saying, "I baptize you in the name of the Father, and of the Son, and of the Holy Spirit." And when he brought that child into the body of Christ through the cosmic waters of the font, it was not his hand, but the hand of Jesus that did so. So who baptized that child? Jesus did!

In fact, Jesus gives His compassionate touch to all people as they pass through the waters of the font. With this compassionate touch comes resurrection for souls from death to sin into a new life in Christ. No dead person can ever bring himself back to life. It is an utter impossibility. Someone else needs to bring life back to dead souls. That person is Jesus. No decisions. No choices. No dead people resurrecting themselves!

Johann Gerhard, the seventeenth-century Lutheran theologian, wrote a book of short meditations. One of these prayers, entitled "Thanksgiving for Conversion," beautifully describes Jesus' work of granting new life to dead sinners. Gerhard writes:

> *O gracious God, I give thanks to You that You converted my hardened heart, which did not know how to repent, and that you removed my heart of stone and gave me a heart of flesh* (Ezekiel 36:26). *I had the power to fall into sin and guilt. I did not have the power to rise to repentance. By my own power I was able to go astray. . . . My soul was born spiritually curved toward sin and earthly things. No human power could correct it. Only Your grace was able to restore my soul so it loved You and desired Your heavenly blessings. . . . You, my God, converted me, and I am converted* (Jeremiah 31:18). *. . . I was dead in sin, and You made me alive. I was able to contribute as much to my conversion as a dead person is able to contribute to his resurrection* (John 6:44; John 11:43). *If You had not drawn me, I would never have come to You.* (*Meditations on Divine Mercy,* pp. 75–76)

Notice in this prayer who is always doing the verbs. It is God who is always doing the action. He converts. He restores the soul. He makes alive. He resurrects. God in Christ is always doing the actions. Just as it is with the young man from Nain, so it is with all people at the font. It is Jesus whose "hallowed touch brought sanctity" ("The Infant Priest Was Holy Born," *LSB* 624:2; *HS98* 853:2).

Resurrection in the Font

What does it mean to be incorporated into the body of Jesus Christ? If what is His is now yours, can anything harm you? Describe the kind of comfort it gives to know that you are indestructible in Jesus.

What is the antidote against death? Where is that medicine of immortality given over and over again?

Jesus touches sinners and, with that hallowed touch, the sinner is cleansed, forgiven, and resurrected. Like touching the bier of the dead young man, Jesus is subjecting Himself to ritual uncleanliness at every Baptism. Thankfully, "death is swallowed up in victory" (1 Corinthians 15:54). In other words, death cannot and will not have dominion over those who are in Christ. Death is defeated at the cross, and life prevails.

Everyone who is baptized is incorporated into that same body of Jesus, the one that hung on the cross and rose from the dead. People are not baptized into a bubble or into a local church, but they are baptized into Christ, who bears life and immortality in His very body. What comfort and confidence this holy Sacrament of Baptism brings, as it unites a person with the death and resurrection of Jesus Christ! In his book on evangelism, *Speaking the Gospel Today*, revised edition, Robert Kolb beautifully describes the power of the cross and resurrection:

> *This message of new creation through Jesus' resurrection delivers the antidote against death and all the warping terror and rage it generates in human life. Because death ends it all, human creatures living in the darkness of its shadow are blinded to life's true meaning. . . . Therefore, for a person plagued by the*

> *meaninglessness of life, a view of life from Golgotha restores a vision of life's meaning in the midst of its seeming senselessness, simply because Golgotha points toward an empty tomb and the corpse of God come back to life.* (p. 173)

When people are in Christ, they are new creations (Galatians 6:15) because they have moved from the destructibleness of the sinful life and being dead on a bier to being totally indestructible as they reside within the precious body of Jesus. Jesus' resurrection is truly the "antidote against death," and that same medicine is repeatedly given at the altar where Christians feast upon the life-giving, resurrected body and blood of Jesus Christ. Certainly, where Jesus is, resurrection and life must prevail. The joy, of course, is that they always do!

Conclusion

As is clearly seen in the story of the widow's son at Nain, God became man for one reason: to give life to all who die. Death is not natural and is not from God. The intention is that all have life and live forever. Thankfully, since death is not natural and not from God, death cannot ever defeat God. Although it may appear for a time that death has won the victory, soon enough, life will prevail.

The story of the widow's son at Nain is really Jesus' story as well, and, because it is Jesus' story, it is also the story of the baptized. The resurrection of this poor son prefigures the resurrection of Jesus Himself. Moreover, it prefigures the resurrection at every baptismal font. The glorious thing is that when it comes to resurrections, it is always Jesus doing the verbs. Human beings have nothing to worry about. Although they are dead to sin, it is God's rich mercy and love that brings new life, that resurrects them from sin to new life in Christ. In the words of Luther, "The significance of Baptism is a blessed dying unto sin and a resurrection in the grace of God, so that the old man, conceived and born in sin, is there drowned, and a new man, born in grace, comes forth and rises" (AE 35:30).

Prayer

We know that Christ is raised and dies
no more.
Embraced by death, He broke its fearful
hold;
And our despair He turned to blazing joy.
Alleluia!

We share by water in His saving death.
Reborn, we share with Him an Easter life
As living members of a living Christ.
Alleluia!

The Father's splendor clothes the Son
with life.
The Spirit's power shakes the Church
of God.
Baptized, we live with God the Three
in One.
Alleluia!
("We Know That Christ Is Raised,"
LSB 603; *HS98* 846)

4 Widow's Son at Nain

Death and Taxes

We live in a day and age when people are trying to avoid death at all cost. Why do you think people want to avoid dying? Have you ever heard that death is "natural" and just a part of life?

Read **Genesis 1 and 2**. In the creation account, is there any talk of death? Is death really "natural"? Yet if people believe that death is "natural," why do they try to avoid it so much? Is there any chance death may not be "natural" but rather a result of sin and a consequence of living in a fallen world?

Death is certainly not foreign to us. It has been said that a person can count on two things: death and taxes! For us, death is sure, but how about for God?

On the Road Again

Read **Luke 7:11–17**. In all of Jesus' moving about, where is His ultimate destination? (See **Luke 9:51**.) What's in Jerusalem that makes it the holy city? Now read **John 2:18–22**. What is going to happen to that temple?

Read **Genesis 22:1–8**. Recall the three-day journey of Isaac to his death on Mount Moriah (the land where Jerusalem would one day be built). How is Isaac's journey a microcosm of Jesus' three-year journey to the cross in Jerusalem?

The widow's son is dead and therefore completely defiled. Jesus is completely holy (see **Acts 4:27** and the reference to "holy servant Jesus") as He is God in the flesh. Why would the God-man, who is completely holy, even come near to that which is unholy and defiled?

How is Jesus' whole life really a confrontation between life and death? Jesus became man at the incarnation for what reason?

What is the status of the woman whom Jesus meets? She is not only lonely because her son is dead, but she is now an outcast. Why? How is Jesus' stopping to help the widow a picture of what He came to this earth to do?

True Compassion

Have you ever experienced the death of a loved one or a loved one of a close friend? Discuss how awkward this type of situation can be, especially when it comes to finding the right words to say.

As members of the body of Christ, it is our duty and privilege to show compassion, since our way is the "Jesus way." Yet this is not always easy, and, frankly, it is impossible. Why?

It is a heresy to say that God is, of His essence, wrathful. Rather, He is loving, compassionate, and so forth. With that said, how is Jesus' compassion different from ours?

A Compassionate Touch

Think of a time when you really just needed a hug, a pat on the back, or a kind handshake. Have you ever noticed how the touch of a loved one can be comforting in a time of distress? Why do you think Jesus does not touch the widow?

In what way does He actually extend His touch to her?

When Jesus touches the bier, is there any chance He will become unclean? How is His touch of the bier actually a picture of the cross?

Read stanza 2 of "The Infant Priest Was Holy Born" (*LSB* 624; *HS98* 853). What is it that "brings sanctity" or holiness to the unholy and defiled?

Read the Augsburg Confession, Article II. How has Jesus stopped our own burial processions?

It's All in the Word

Listen to the quote from the writings of Martin Luther. Was Jesus active and working at creation? In what way? How does that Word still speak to this day?

Read the following:
Genesis 1:1–3
Psalm 29
Mark 1:40–45
John 11:38–44
Matthew 26:26–29
What happens when the Lord speaks? Does He speak realities, that is, do things do what He tells them to do? What does He say to the widow's son at Nain? What is the result of that Word?

Moving to the Font

If you had to describe our sinful condition, what words would you use? Given what you know about the disease of sin, how do you compare to the widow's son at Nain? How are you dead?

If you are dead, is there any chance that you can bring yourself back to life? Since bringing yourself back is an utter impossibility, who has to do it for you? How does He do it?

Read Luther's Small Catechism on Holy Baptism, part two. How is Jesus' resurrection of the widow's son at Nain a picture of what happens at every baptismal font? Who is it that meets you at the font?

Compassion and Touch at the Font

Jesus meets dead sinners at the font to baptize them and give them life. For what reason does He do this? How is Jesus' yearning for you even deeper than that of a mother yearning for her child?

Examine the service of Holy Baptism (*LSB*, p. 268; *LW*, p. 199). In what ways does the pastor resemble Jesus Christ in this account of the widow's son at Nain? Any moving? Any speaking? Any touching? Any language of "new life"?

Listen to Gerhard's "Thanksgiving for Conversion" prayer. Often people have trouble admitting that they are spiritually dead and unable to bring themselves back to life. Why is this so? Is it hard to give the glory and honor to someone else? Yet in the act of salvation or conversion, who always does the verbs? Who brings life and resurrection to dead sinners at the font?

Resurrection in the Font

What does it mean to be incorporated into the body of Jesus Christ? If what is His is now yours, can anything harm you? Describe the kind of comfort it gives to know that you are indestructible in Jesus.

What is the antidote against death? Where is that medicine of immortality given over and over again?

5

Lazarus

Lesson Focus

Apart from His own resurrection on the eighth day, the day of the new creation, the resurrection of Lazarus has often been considered one of Christ's greatest miracles during His earthly life. This is not to say that the other miracles are of less importance. Rather, the similarities between the resurrection of Lazarus and the resurrection of Jesus Christ are so great that one can hardly see the difference.

Gospel Focus

In the historic one-year lectionary, the account of Lazarus' resurrection is the Gospel reading for Easter evening. The resurrection of Lazarus gives the reader a foretaste of the feast (Jesus' own resurrection) to come. It reflects forward upon the glorious mystery of Jesus' resurrection on the eighth day—Easter Sunday—and subsequently, the resurrection of all flesh on the Last Day.

Prayer

The strife is o'er, the battle done.
Now is the victor's triumph won;
Now be the song of praise begun.
Alleluia!

The pow'rs of death have done their worst,
But Christ their legions hath dispersed.
Let shouts of holy joy outburst.
Alleluia!
("The Strife Is O'er, the Battle Done," *LSB* 464:1–2; *LW* 143:1–2)

Introduction

Read Genesis 1:26–27. God created man in His own image. How is our rebellion a "cosmic rebellion"? What changes with the fall into sin?

What is the greater cosmic event: the fall or the redemption? Discuss.

In his book on apologetics *The Defense Never Rests: A Lawyer's Quest for the Gospel*, Craig Parton says:

> *If God was indeed to become man and give us insight into one issue, it would be on the enigma of death. In Jesus Christ we find the announcement that we have brought about our own doom by our cosmic rebellion against God, but that God has acted to deal with the separation created by man when man was wholly incapable of effecting such a reconciliation. Jesus claimed to come to earth to deal with man's sin ("For the Son of Man came to seek and to save what was lost" [Luke 19:10]) and to give a final answer to death for all who will believe.* (p. 91)

"The enigma of death" and "cosmic rebellion" are code words for an eschatological event, one with "end times" implications, that changes the course of history forever. The fall into sin is a "cosmic rebellion" in that the image of God is lost and creation is condemned. Similarly, the incarnation of Jesus Christ is an eschatological event, in that it changes history and eternity forever. Nothing is the same when God breaks on the scene and begins "to deal with the separation created by man when man was wholly incapable of effecting such a reconciliation." The great revelation of Jesus Christ, or the apocalypse (from *apocalypto*, "to reveal"), provides the pattern of what is to come. From His incarnation on, everything that Jesus does is cosmic in nature, the greatest of which is His bitter suffering, death, and victorious resurrection. The salvific work of Jesus far outweighs the fall into sin on the "cosmic scale." Moreover, the account of the resurrection of Lazarus provides a deeper glimpse into the cosmic, eschatological nature of what Jesus is about to do in Jerusalem—die for the sins of the world and be raised for the life of the world. This is but a foretaste of the good things to come!

What a Friend

How is thinking of Jesus as a "good bud" or a mean judge not quite accurate?

The two natures of Christ is a great mystery, but how does John 3:6 help us to understand it a bit better?

Read the Apostles' Creed. How is the Trinity an icon of a relationship? How are the persons of the Trinity related to one another? How is the Trinity a family?

It is often hard to think of Jesus as a friend. Most people usually fall on one end or the other of the "Buddy Jesus" spectrum. Some think of Jesus as a good buddy who is there to laugh and chat and sing and play. To them, He is nothing more than the good friend next door. He is certainly not God. He certainly does not need to do something gory like shed His blood and die. No, He is just a good listener—always there when needed. For others, there is the idea that Jesus is off in heaven, not concerned about relationships or people or fleshly things. He is certainly not a buddy Jesus, but rather is utterly disconnected from His creation. He is no friend, but an omniscient (all-knowing) and omnipotent (all-powerful) judge.

Whether one thinks of Jesus as a best bud or an authoritative judge makes no difference. Essentially, neither is correct. Jesus is substantially two natures, God and man. He is substantially, as Luther describes, "true God, begotten of the Father from eternity," but He is also substantially "true man, born of the Virgin Mary" (Explanation of Second Article). The apostle John beat Luther to the punch when he said, "That which is born of the flesh is flesh, and that which is born of the Spirit is spirit" (John 3:6). This simple verse is a clear confession of the two natures in the one person, Jesus Christ. From the flesh of the Virgin Mary Jesus receives His flesh (human nature), and from the Father He receives His Spirit (divine nature). There are two natures in Christ; that point must never be forgotten.

Since there are two natures in Christ, He, at the same moment, has complete control over creation and is able to sympathize with all that one must bear and endure. Therefore, it is not unwarranted that the sisters, Mary and Martha, send for Jesus with the words, "Lord, he whom You love is ill" (John 11:3). That statement alone is quite fascinating. "He whom You love" is a clear indication that Jesus is all about relationships. In fact the very nature of the Holy Trinity is relational. The Father is eternal. The Son is begotten of the Father from all eternity. The Holy Spirit proceeds from the Father and the Son. Father, Son, begotten, and proceeds are key words for a relationship. Moreover, they indicate a familial relationship that is defined by love. The great thing about Jesus is that He longs to replicate the relationship of the Holy Trinity with all people on earth by bringing them into relationship with the Holy Trinity. Baptism is that great entrance into God. When people are baptized "into Christ Jesus" (Romans 6:3), they are baptized into the physical body of Jesus, which then puts them into a relationship with the Trinity. All that Jesus has, He gives to His children. He holds nothing back from them. Even more, when Jesus acts by giving His gifts, He not only gives Himself, but He gives all of the Godhead, for what one person (Father, Son, or Holy Spirit) is doing, all persons are doing. With that said, Jesus is wholly about relationships, the giving of Himself, and infinite, divine love. Jesus has a divine relationship with Lazarus, and He shows divine love toward him.

Death: Eternal or Temporal?

Read John 11:1–44. All things being equal, why is it easier to understand Jesus' statement, "This illness does not lead to death," as referring to eternal death?

Since Jesus is love in the flesh, and of His nature He can show only love, Jesus says in response to the grave news about Lazarus, "This illness does not lead to death" (John 11:4). This statement can really be taken two ways. Either Jesus means that Lazarus's illness will not lead to eternal death in hell, or He means that it will not lead to physical death on earth. With a cursory read of the text, it appears that Jesus is talking about the former. It is almost as though Jesus is saying, "Yes, he will die physically, but he will not die forever." How is this so? Just look at how long it takes Jesus to get to Lazarus. If Jesus really means that Lazarus will not die physically, one would think that Jesus would make haste to get to Lazarus and heal him from his illness. Rather, Jesus stays two additional days before finally heading toward Bethany. He does, however, promise that this illness "is for the glory of God, so that the Son of God may be glorified through it" (John 11:4). So just how will Jesus find glory in letting a good friend die?

The Sleep of Death

Have you ever gone to bed worried that you might not wake up? Does falling asleep at night usually presuppose waking up in the morning? How could the language of Lazarus having "fallen asleep" have been confusing for the disciples?

Discuss why Jesus said He was glad not to be there when Lazarus died. If Jesus had healed Lazarus, would He have had the chance to resurrect him?

Think about and discuss how death is like a sleep. How are people awakened from death to new life?

After two days, Jesus decides it is time to go to Judea and do something for His ailing, now dead, friend. After baffling the disciples with the desire to return to the place where the Jews were trying to stone Him (John 11:8), Jesus tells the disciples His reason for returning. "Our friend Lazarus has fallen asleep, but I go to awaken him" (John 11:11). It is interesting that Jesus uses the language of sleep here. Just as "burial in the great fish" presupposes a resurrection, so "Lazarus has fallen asleep" presupposes an awakening. Still, the disciples do not understand the Lord's babbling. As the text says, "Now Jesus had spoken of his death, but they thought that He meant taking rest in sleep" (John 11:13). So Jesus clears it up for the disciples. "Then Jesus said to them plainly, 'Lazarus has died'" (John 11:14). Jesus tells them frankly that a man whom He cares for and dearly loves is dead. It really cannot get any clearer. Jesus is too late. No chance of saving His friend from physical death. He must mean that Lazarus's illness is not one that will lead to eternal death, right?

What comes next is telling. "And for your sake, I am glad that I was not there, so that you may believe" (John 11:15), Jesus says. Harsh words from such a good friend of Lazarus. "I am glad that I was not there." How much more cruel and disheartening can Jesus be? But with Jesus, everything occurs for a reason. It is not that He wants His friend to die. Rather, Jesus knows that when His friend dies, He will then have the opportunity to awaken him. Death is but a sleep, and Jesus is ready and able to move into action and bring life to, or awaken, His dear friend, Lazarus. All of this happens so that the disciples might believe.

If Jesus comes to an ailing Lazarus, He can make him well. But since Jesus is coming to a dead Lazarus, He can do much more than give him temporal health. Jesus can resurrect him! This resurrection is crucial for the disciples' faith as well as the faith of all Christians. If Jesus does not bring or cannot bring Lazarus back from the dead, then who is to say that He can bring Himself back from the dead? After all, it is the "Son" who "gives life to whom He will" (5:21). Yet if He is unsuccessful in giving life to others, no one will ever believe that He can bring Himself back from the dead.

Like Lazarus, all sinners live in a sort of "sleep of death." Like the foolish virgins (Matthew 25:1–13), they are not prepared for the

Christ. In other words, they need to be awakened and ready for the coming of the Christ. Thankfully, that is what Baptism does. It awakens! It opens drowsy eyes asleep in sin to see the Messiah, the very Lamb of God, Jesus Christ, and, when a person sees Christ for who He is, there is only life and salvation.

But He Is Really Dead!

It appeared that Jesus did not make much of an effort to get to Lazarus. Discuss what it must have been like for Mary and Martha as the last ounce of hope seeped away, and Lazarus passed from the third day to the fourth.

When Jesus arrived on the fourth day, what appeared to have won, death or life? Why? What emotions do you think Mary and Martha were experiencing at this time?

Why does Jesus' statement, "Your brother will rise again" (John 11:23), sound so foolish?

What is the ultimate reason for Jesus' coming into this world? How does He do it? Where and how are you made new?

After Jesus explains the true meaning of "sleep" to His disciples, He is off to find His friend Lazarus. One would think that Jesus would be quick to find this dear friend of His, but it appears that Jesus is a few days too late. "Lazarus had already been in the tomb four days" (John 11:17). To the average reader, it is very clear that Lazarus is dead. Four days in a tomb is a lifetime for the bereaved and certainly too late for any revivals. Especially for the Jews, however, this is a terrible reality. The footnote in the Concordia Self-Study Bible for verse 17 states: "Many Jews believed that the soul remained near the body for three days after death in the hope of returning to it. If this idea was in the minds of these people, they obviously thought all hope was gone—Lazarus was irrevocably dead" (p. 1628). If this is true, then Jesus was just a day late. One day earlier, and those mourning Lazarus's death would have had some hope of a resurrection, no matter how dim it may have been. However, the third day was no longer. Lazarus was officially dead, with no hope of a return to life.

From this, it is clear why Martha met Jesus with the words, "Lord, if You had been here, my brother would not have died" (John 11:21). True, if Jesus had come with haste when He heard of Lazarus's illness, He might have been able to heal Lazarus before the onset of death. Even more, if Jesus had just arrived a day earlier than He actually did, instead of staying put, He might have been able to bring Lazarus back to life, even after death. Yet, in response to Martha's statement, Jesus showed that He is in control of both death and life, and no amount of time can thwart His power to raise the dead and give new life. Jesus said to Martha, "Your brother will rise again" (John 11:23). Knowing her Scriptures and her Lord well, Martha responded, "I know that he will rise again in the resurrection on the last day" (John 11:24). However, that was not what she was upset about.

Martha knew that her beloved brother, Lazarus, would rise again when Christ returns on the Last Day. She certainly knew that one day there will be a resurrection of the flesh and her brother will be included. But, in the meantime, that did not help her grief. Her brother was still dead. It was still the fourth day. Hope was still gone. Or was it?

Resurrection: Now, Not Yet

With the statement, "I am the resurrection and the life. Whoever believes in Me, though he die, yet shall he live, and everyone who lives and believes in Me shall never die" (John 11:25–26), how did Jesus address both Lazarus and Martha?

Why is it important that the attention be on Jesus? Apart from Him, can any life be granted?

What makes Jesus the life giver? Is it His raising of others, or His own resurrection?

Discuss how Martha encountered life incarnate.

How is the binding of Lazarus symbolic of sin? What is symbolized in the unbinding? In response to poor Martha, Jesus said, "I am the resurrection and the life. Whoever believes in Me, though he die, yet shall he live, and everyone who lives and believes in Me shall never die" (John 11:25–26). Notice how Jesus took the attention off of Lazarus and the grieving women and placed it upon Himself. Moreover, in this statement, Jesus addressed both dead Lazarus and living Martha. "Whoever believes in Me, though he die, yet shall he live" refers to Lazarus. Lazarus was dead, but he will live eternally. Death is not the end of him. There is certainly more to come. Next, Jesus addressed Martha and all other living believers with the words, "And everyone who lives and believes in Me shall never die." Martha and those mourning the loss of Lazarus were physically alive. Moreover, they believed in Jesus Christ. Therefore, like Lazarus, they will never die (eternally).

What Jesus did in these two verses was to put Himself at the center of the resurrection. Apart from Him, there is no resurrection, neither for those who have already died, nor for those who will one day die. This is because Jesus is, of His essence, resurrection and life. Therefore, those who believe in Jesus, whether dead or alive, have resurrection and life in hand. Some call this the great "now, not yet" of Jesus. The "not yet" is that certainly those still living have not experienced the resurrection of their own flesh. Moreover, Lazarus is still lying dead in a grave. The "now," however, is that, since Jesus is there, they have the resurrection in their midst, and the sure and certain hope of the life to come. They have the resurrection, now and not yet.

This idea of Jesus being the resurrection and the life, in and of Himself, is furthered by the theology of a certain icon. An icon often called "Christ the Life Giver" is a simple image of Jesus blessing with His right hand and holding an open book in the other with the words, "I am the resurrection and the life. Whoever believes in Me, though he die, yet shall he live, and everyone who lives and believes in Me shall never die" from John 11 written in the open book. At first glance, this is quite strange. One would tend to think that an icon of the life giver, along with these words from the Gospel, would include a picture of an empty tomb or Jesus' own resurrection. But that is the significance of Jesus' words and the idea of the "now, not yet."

Jesus is not the resurrection and the life because He rises from the dead Himself. In other words, His own resurrection is not what precipitates Him calling Himself the resurrection and the life. Rather, He rises from the dead Himself, and brings others back to life, because He is the resurrection and the life incarnate. Therefore, contained in that simple icon of Jesus is, in actuality, an icon of the resurrection and the life, and that is precisely who Martha encountered in this text.

When Jesus said, "Your brother will rise again" (John 11:23), the question was "When will he rise, then or now?" And the answer was, "Yes!" Lazarus will rise again when Christ returns—as St. Paul says, "Behold! I tell you a mystery. We shall not all sleep, but we shall all be changed, in a moment, in the twinkling of an eye, at the last trumpet. For the trumpet will sound, and the dead will be raised imperishable, and we shall be changed" (1 Corinthians 15:51–52). However, Lazarus also rose again that day, as Jesus Christ, the resurrection and the life, came to meet his dead body head-on.

Beyond Expectations

This was not Jesus' first miracle. He'd healed many, turned water to wine, given bread for thousands, yet it did not cross Martha's mind that Jesus might actually be able to bring her brother back from the dead. Why?

Why does Jesus not like the question "How?"

In response to Jesus' promise that "Your brother will rise again" (John 11:23), Martha did not give Jesus enough credit. However, she did not doubt the resurrection of all flesh on the Last Day. Martha knew that day was coming and she knew her brother will be raised. She also, however, believed that her brother would remain dead in the grave until that time. But with Jesus, there is always more! He is always ready to go far beyond one's imagination and understanding. It is almost like the Jews asking Jesus in John 6, "How can this man give us His flesh to eat?" That's the wrong question. According to human reason and intellect, it is unthinkable that a man could give his flesh as food. It is also unthinkable that one could be raised before the Last Day. "How can Jesus do this?" Martha is probably thinking.

"How?" is precisely the question that Jesus rebels against. One can never say that Christ would not or could not. He works when and where and how He pleases, all according to His good pleasure. So when Martha said, "I know that he will rise again in the resurrection on the last day" (John 11:24), she essentially asked, "How?" Again, that is the question that Jesus looks to destroy. He is the resurrection and the life, and if He so chooses, He can, with a word, bring that dead body back to life. Jesus is always there to give, not take. He is always there to bestow His good gifts, and those gifts always keep on giving. There is always more to Christ! In fact, just when one thinks Christ has given or done all He can give or do, He inevitably far exceeds human expectations! That is, of course, the way of Christ. Always giving more and never expecting anything in return.

A True Friend

Read stanza 2 of "My Song Is Love Unknown." Jesus is a dear friend because of what He gives to people. Just what is it He gives?

How does Jesus bestow that gift? What must He do in order to be a dear friend?

As mentioned earlier, it is often difficult to have a correct understanding of Jesus as "friend." He either ends up being a "Buddy Jesus" or the "big guy in the sky." What is fascinating about this account of Lazarus's death and resurrection is that it clearly shows the two natures of Christ (divine and human) in the one person, as Christ shows His power over death and love of a friend. One of the great hymns of Lent helps to bring this idea out a bit more. Stanza 2 of "My Song Is Love Unknown" reads:

He came from His blest throne
Salvation to bestow;
But men made strange, and none
The longed for Christ would know.
But, oh, my friend,
My friend indeed,
Who at my need
His life did spend!
(*LSB* 430:2; *LW* 91:2)

God comes down from heaven in the person of Jesus Christ ("He came from His blest throne") and invades our creation. He comes here to dress Himself with a robe of flesh and blood, and, in that flesh and blood, to die for the sins of the world. This is the God-man, Jesus Christ, but more, He is also a dear friend who does everything from bear the brutal beating of the Romans, and die a gruesome death on Calvary, to weep with those who mourn the death of a loved one. What an amazing thing, that God in the flesh dies for all and cries with all.

It is this same Jesus who was caught up in the emotion of Mary's arrival. She met Jesus, falling to His feet in an act of utter submission and worship, saying, "Lord, if You had been here, my brother would not have died" (John 11:32). The same plea from both sisters shows that, to a certain extent, they got it! They understood that Jesus is God in the flesh, and He alone possesses the power to raise their dead brother. However, Mary's words do not show the same hope for the final resurrection that Martha's do.

This does not necessarily mean that she did not believe in the final resurrection, but she certainly did not express that hope when she conversed with Jesus. Moreover, neither of the sisters said, "Lord, now that You are here, You can raise Lazarus." In their minds, all hope was gone for now. Four days had passed and the time for weeping had begun.

Anger and Indignation at the Enemy

What caused Mary and the Jews to weep? Why did Christ get angry? At what were His anger and indignation directed?

How does Jesus' being troubled at Lazarus' death foreshadow the troubling at His own death? How does His being troubled show the depth of His friendship?

Upon seeing the weeping Mary, along with all the Jews who also were weeping, Jesus was "deeply moved in His spirit and greatly troubled" (John 11:33). The Greek word for greatly moved, *ene-brimasato*, is one of anger or indignation. It is more than just merely being upset. One could say that Jesus was angered in His spirit. But what was Jesus angry about? He was certainly not upset with the sisters, was He? He was certainly not upset that many were mourning Lazarus's death. Rather, "He was strongly agitated over the power which the enemy of mankind, death, was here exhibiting over human beings" (*Kretzmann*, p. 474). He was agitated that the old dreadful foe, Satan, seemed to have another reason to rejoice. He was agitated that death had not yet been vanquished. The forces from below, that is, from the devil, caused Jesus deep agitation and indignation. Jesus was, as the text says, "deeply moved."

In addition to being agitated over the power of death, Jesus was also "greatly troubled" (John 11:33). Interestingly enough, this word for troubled (*tarasso*) is one that has physical connotations. To be greatly troubled is to be stirred or shaken up, possibly even physically. Moreover, this is the exact same word that Jesus used following the triumphal entry on Palm Sunday when confronting His death. Jesus said, "Now is My soul troubled. And what shall I say? 'Father, save Me from this hour'? But for this purpose I have come to this hour" (John 12:27). Jesus' purpose is to die for the sins of the world. That is His purpose: to redeem this lost and condemned world, and make it completely new. However, the way to this redemption and new creation is only through death. Just as it was a friend's death that troubled Him in John 11, so it was His own death that brought Him trouble in chapter 12. But what a friend one has in Jesus! In His being "greatly troubled," Jesus showed that He cares for His friends just as much, if not more, than He cares for Himself.

Death Is Not Natural

In what way does Mary's weeping compare with the weeping that goes on in hell (see Matthew 8:12)? Discuss how weeping is a by-product of the fall.

Jesus' own death and resurrection is in the near-distant future. Explain how Jesus' movement toward death (John 11:38) prefigures His own walk to death at Golgotha?

Jesus being "deeply moved in His spirit and greatly troubled" (11:33) was a result of the death of a dear friend and the ensuing tears that flowed from Mary's eyes. But Mary was not simply shedding a tear or two. Rather, she was, as the text says, "weeping." The word for weeping here (*klaio*) is one that connotes loud wailing or nearly screaming. Given the Greek word, this "weeping" appears to be nearly uncontrollable. Moreover, it is this kind of uncontrollable weeping that is found in hell. Jesus, when He speaks of hell in Matthew 8:12, says, "In that place there will be weeping and gnashing of teeth." Strangely enough, weeping is what occurs in hell and also what occurs here at the death of Lazarus. Why is this so?

Weeping is a thing of hell and should be foreign to this creation. It is not right that people weep over the loss of a loved one because death is not natural. People are not meant to die. In the glorious Garden of Eden, there were just life and joy and happiness and peace. Certainly no weeping! But with the fall came death and with death came weeping. Because sin entered the world, the powers from hell now have a grip on this creation and all that is in it. In the words of Kretzmann, "Death is a cruel enemy, for in a moment he destroys the happiness of families and friends, and rends the closest ties asunder" (p. 474). Yes, death is a cruel enemy, and the force behind death is the great deceiver of mankind, Satan. His deception leads to sin, sin to death, and death to weeping. But, once more, this is not the way things are supposed to be!

With death and hell appearing to win the day, Jesus asked, "Where have you laid him?" (John 11:34). He was about to seek out death and destroy it with a word. He was about to bring life and immortality to light, even amid the darkness of this desperate situation. Like the widow's son at Nain, one can imagine the scene as Jesus made His way to the place of burial. Life incarnate was about to meet death head-on. But as He made His way to death, the strangest thing happened. Jesus began to shed tears. "Jesus wept" (John 11:35), the text says. As some are quick to point out, this is the shortest verse in all of Holy Scripture. However, there is much packed into these two words. This is not the uncontrollable weeping that Mary exhibited when she met Jesus. Rather this weeping (*dak-roo-o*) was the heartfelt shedding of tears over the loss of a friend. Moreover, this was the heartfelt shedding of tears over the pain that death causes. Yes, Jesus was grieving the loss of Lazarus, but, more than that, He was saddened by the great power of death itself. Keep in mind, the resurrection that was about to occur was not long before Jesus' own passion, death, and resurrection. One can see that Jesus was upset over death, but also eager to get the job done. He was eager to slay the power of death forever.

The Word Is in Control

Often at a funeral, the family of the deceased finds it difficult to function and even make rational decisions. This is completely understandable, but it also necessitates that someone be there to help the bereaved through those difficult days. Simply put, the bereaved need someone to take control of their lives because death is powerful enough to make people lose control. In a similar way, Jesus came to the tomb of Lazarus and demonstrated that He was in total control of the situation. Jesus directed the situation from the very beginning with, "Take away the stone" (John 11:39). Up until this point, death had controlled everything. It had caused traveling and tears. Yet Life Himself was taking control and showing that He has full dominion over all, even death itself!

Yet even amid Jesus taking full control of the situation, dear Martha, who kept house while Jesus visited and worked while He would have her only listen, once again wanted to make sure nothing unpleasant surrounded Jesus' visit to the tomb of her brother. "Lord, by this time there will be an odor, for he has been dead four days" (John 11:39). Yes, she was probably right. Lazarus would probably smell a bit. However, none of that stopped Jesus. The one who touches lepers and the unclean is not afraid of an odor. He was ready to defeat death with a word.

Glory in Death?

Where do most people try and find the look of God? What are some examples in the life of Jesus where most would pinpoint His glory? Where is His glory *truly* to be found?

Knowing all of that, why was Jesus going to raise Lazarus from the dead? What is it supposed to be a picture of?

How can Christians have the peculiarity of "glory in death"?

What are some ways Jesus did the unexpected in this account?

When speaking of Lazarus' illness, Jesus said in verse 4, "It is for the glory of God, so that the Son of God may be glorified through it." Now the time was here. Jesus reminded Martha with the words, "Did I not tell you that if you believed you would see the glory of God?" (John 11:40). The question is: what is the glory of God? Many think that God's glory is seen in magnificent and wonderful things like miracles or healings. But one who deserves glory deserves it because they have done something of distinction. Because they have done something that no one else can do. Even Satan can do wonderful and mighty things, but there is one thing unique to the God-man, Jesus Christ.

Only Jesus Christ can die for the sins of the world and rise again on the eighth day, making all things new. Jesus did not raise Lazarus from the dead in order to gain fame and majesty. Rather, He raised Lazarus from the dead because Lazarus was the foretaste or icon of the great death and resurrection to come. This resurrection was truly "for the glory of God" because it would prefigure the glory of God that is found in Jesus' own passion, death, and resurrection.

In the coming chapters, Jesus will mention the word *glory* a number of times, all of them referring to His impending death. It is a strange thing, though, that glory is seen in the most shameful of circumstances. However, Jesus never does things according to human understanding. Usually, everything is reversed. The Great Shepherd becomes a Lamb. The great High Priest becomes the sacrifice. An apparent defeat on the cross becomes a victory. A shameful experience is actually one of glory. With Jesus, nothing is as it seems, not even a man who is as good as dead, for he would soon rise.

With all this talk about glory, one would expect the resurrection of Lazarus to be a "glorious" one. One would expect Jesus to move in like a magical, dramatic healer putting on a show for those around. However, one will soon see that the glorious things of God are not the same as those of men. The impending resurrection will not appear glorious at all, in fact, it will even look a bit shameful. Lazarus will come out still wearing the clothes and odor of death. But that is the Jesus way! The normal, everyday, and even shameful turns out to be the most glorious of all.

The Sent One

Why is it important that Jesus be the "Sent One"? If He is not sent by the Father, as Luther says in his hymn, then what is He? Does Jesus have any credibility apart from the Father?

Read stanza 5 of "Dear Christians, One and All, Rejoice." Why was Jesus sent?

How did Jesus go further than all those not sent by the Father, and thereby validate all His miracles, especially this resurrection?

After speaking of His glory and having the stone removed, Jesus continued with a rather peculiar statement: "Father, I thank You that You have heard Me. I knew that You always hear Me, but I said this on account of the people standing around, that they may believe that You sent Me" (John 11:41–42). Jesus spoke to the Father in order that others might know He is the "Sent One." If Jesus is not sent from the Father, then He is a lunatic who is skilled in magic and the things of the devil. But if He is sent from the Father, then He is fully capable of showing mercy and love to this sinful world. Moreover, "the reason why Christ loves sinners is that His Father commanded Him to do so" (AE 51:47). In Luther's hymn "Dear Christians, One and All, Rejoice," he speaks of the "Sent One," His sending, and the reason for that sending:

God said to His beloved Son:
"It's time to have compassion.
Then go, bright jewel of My crown,
And bring to all salvation;
From sin and sorrow set them free;
Slay bitter death for them that they
May live with You forever."
(*LSB* 556:5; *LW* 353:5)

Jesus was about to show compassion and raise a dead man because that is what the "Sent One" is sent to do. A lunatic would stop at the raising. However, Jesus validated His mission through His own bitter suffering, death, and resurrection. Once again, this resurrection was but a foretaste of the good things to come.

The Voice

Often one of the most stressful and time-consuming tasks before having a child is deciding on a name. Yet from the moment the child comes out of the womb, parents and family waste no time, and instantly start calling him or her by that name. But when does a person really receive their name? What is the job of the Good Shepherd when it comes to those named ones? Explain how the sequence of naming, calling, and new life/resurrection is displayed at every baptismal font.

How is the binding of Lazarus symbolic of sin? What is symbolized in the unbinding?

What is the ultimate reason for Jesus' coming into this world? How does He do it? Where and how are you made new?

Once again, Jesus speaks. "Lazarus, come out." As Kretzmann translates it (p. 475), "Hither out!" And what happens? Once again, Kretzmann beautifully says:

And the almighty word caused the miracle to happen, brought the man upon whom the process of decay had begun back to life, and gave him the strength to leave the grave, though he was still bound with the customary grave-clothes and had his face covered with a sudary [handkerchief]. (*Kretzmann,* p. 475)

Jesus spoke and it happened! What happened? The cosmos was altered and death was transformed into life. The Word made flesh speaks, and when He does, life rules the day.

It is also fascinating that Jesus called Lazarus by name. This should instantly remind one of the Good Shepherd discourse in John 10. There Jesus says, "The sheep hear His voice, and He calls His own sheep by name and leads them out" (v. 3). Lazarus is one of His own sheep, named in the waters of Baptism. The job of the shepherd is to care for all sheep, no matter if they are sick, hurt, wandering, or even dead. In this instance, one of the Good Shepherd's beloved sheep is now asleep, but, with His voice, the Good Shepherd can bring any sheep from the darkness of death into the light of life.

This rhythm of naming, calling, and new life is precisely what happens at every baptismal font. It is tradition to not give a child their name until their Baptism since they essentially have no name or identity outside of their name and identity in Jesus Christ. However, once they have been incorporated into the body of Christ they are given a name and bear the identity of the Good Shepherd who calls them. And when the Good Shepherd names a person and calls them in the font, they have nothing less than resurrection life!

Finally, Jesus told those tending to the now resurrected Lazarus, "Unbind him, and let him go" (John 11:44). Luther sees this as more than a functional unbinding, which it certainly is, but also as a picture of what Jesus does to every sinner. He says that dead Lazarus "signifies those who are so entangled in sin that they go beyond all bounds; they drift into a habit [of sinning] which then becomes their very nature. They know nothing but sin; they stink and are buried in sin" (AE 51:45). Death and binding provide a picture of every sinner, dead in transgressions and bound in sin. Yet, when the Lord gets involved, it is all free gift, new life, and resurrection!

Jesus comes to this world for one reason: to make all things new! He does this by redeeming mortal, sinful, icky human beings. He takes on flesh and blood that is destined for death and the grave, and makes it new, resurrects it, by taking it into Himself. At the font, sinful human beings are taken, flesh and blood, into the body of Jesus, and given nothing less than true resurrection as they are joined to a perfect body.

Conclusion

There are two key themes throughout the Scriptures that are always at odds with each other: death and resurrection. Death has dominion over this fallen world. Since death has dominion, all sin and all will die. But thanks be to Jesus Christ, who comes to this world with only life and immortality. He shows that life-giving power in the resurrection of Lazarus, which is an icon of His own glorious resurrection. Moreover, it is an icon of every Christian's resurrection from death in sin to new life in Jesus Christ.

Although it is hard to fathom, death will not have the last word. Yes, people still die, but ultimately the victory over death and the grave has been won by Jesus Christ. His death and resurrection are given to all sinners who are incorporated into His body in Holy Baptism. What is His is theirs! Now, when the last hour comes for Christians, there can be confidence that death is truly just a short sleep, and soon Christ will return to raise their baptized bodies to perfection for eternity.

Closing Prayer

Lo, Judah's Lion wins the strife
And conquers death to give us life.
Alleluia!
Come join in joyful praises!

The pow'r of death He broke in two
When He arose to life anew.
Alleluia!
To Him all praise be given!

He frees the prisoned and oppressed
And pardons all whom sin possessed.
Alleluia!
Oh, praise Him for His mercy!

Praise God, all-holy and triune,
For this all-gracious, glorious boon;
Alleluia!
Now gladly sing we Amen.
("Lo, Judah's Lion Wins the Strife,"
LW 146:1, 5, 6, 8)

5

Lazarus

Introduction

Read **Genesis 1:26–27**. God created man in His own image. How is our rebellion a "cosmic rebellion"? What changes with the fall into sin?

What is the greater cosmic event: the fall or the redemption? Discuss.

What a Friend

How is thinking of Jesus as a "good bud" or a mean judge not quite accurate?

The two natures of Christ is a great mystery, but how does **John 3:6** help us to understand it a bit better?

Read the Apostles' Creed. How is the Trinity an icon of a relationship? How are the persons of the Trinity related to one another? How is the Trinity a family?

Death: Eternal or Temporal?

Read **John 11:1–44**. All things being equal, why is it easier to understand Jesus' statement, "This illness does not lead to death," as referring to eternal death?

The Sleep of Death

Have you ever gone to bed worried that you might not wake up? Does falling asleep at night usually presuppose waking up in the morning? How could the language of Lazarus having "fallen asleep" have been confusing for the disciples?

Discuss why Jesus said He was glad not to be there when Lazarus died. If Jesus had healed Lazarus, would He have had the chance to resurrect him?

Think about and discuss how death is like a sleep. How are people awakened from death to new life?

But He Is Really Dead!

It appeared that Jesus did not make much of an effort to get to Lazarus. Discuss what it must have been like for Mary and Martha as the last ounce of hope seeped away, and Lazarus passed from the third day to the fourth.

When Jesus arrived on the fourth day, what appeared to have won, death or life? Why? What emotions do you think Mary and Martha were experiencing at this time?

Why does Jesus' statement, "Your brother will rise again" (**John 11:23**), sound so foolish?

What is the ultimate reason for Jesus' coming into this world? How does He do it? Where and how are you made new?

Resurrection: Now, Not Yet

With the statement, "I am the resurrection and the life. Whoever believes in Me, though he die, yet shall he live, and everyone who lives and believes in Me shall never die" (**John 11:25–26**), how did Jesus address both Lazarus and Martha?

Why is it important that the attention be on Jesus? Apart from Him, can any life be granted?

What makes Jesus the life giver? Is it His raising of others, or His own resurrection?

Discuss how Martha encountered life incarnate.

Beyond Expectations

This was not Jesus' first miracle. He'd healed many, turned water to wine, given bread for thousands, yet it did not cross Martha's mind that Jesus might actually be able to bring her brother back from the dead. Why?

Why does Jesus not like the question "How?"

A True Friend

Read stanza 2 of "My Song Is Love Unknown." Jesus is a dear friend because of what He gives to people. Just what is it He gives?

He came from His blest throne
Salvation to bestow;
But men made strange, and none
The longed for Christ would know.
But, oh, my friend,
My friend indeed,
Who at my need
His life did spend!
(*LSB* 430:2; *LW* 91:2)

How does Jesus bestow that gift? What must He do in order to be a dear friend?

Anger and Indignation at the Enemy

What caused Mary and the Jews to weep? Why did Christ get angry? At what were His anger and indignation directed?

How does Jesus' being troubled at Lazarus's death foreshadow the troubling at His own death? How does His being troubled show the depth of His friendship?

Death Is Not Natural

In what way does Mary's weeping compare with the weeping that goes on in hell (see **Matthew 8:12**)? Discuss how weeping is a by-product of the fall.

Jesus' own death and resurrection is in the near-distant future. Explain how Jesus' movement toward death (**John 11:38**) prefigures His own walk to death at Golgotha?

Glory in Death?

Where do most people try and find the look of God? What are some examples in the life of Jesus where most would pinpoint His glory? Where is His glory truly to be found?

Knowing all of that, why was Jesus going to raise Lazarus from the dead? What is it supposed to be a picture of?

How can Christians have the peculiarity of "glory in death"?

What are some ways Jesus did the unexpected in this account?

The Sent One

Why is it important that Jesus be the "Sent One"? If He is not sent by the Father, as Luther says in his hymn, then what is He? Does Jesus have any credibility apart from the Father?

Read stanza 5 of "Dear Christians, One and All, Rejoice." Why was Jesus sent?

God said to His beloved Son:
"It's time to have compassion.
Then go, bright jewel of My crown,
And bring to all salvation;
From sin and sorrow set them free;
Slay bitter death for them that they
May live with You forever."
(*LSB* 556:5; *LW* 353:5)

How did Jesus go further than all those not sent by the Father, and thereby validate all His miracles, especially this resurrection?

The Voice

Often one of the most stressful and time-consuming tasks before having a child is deciding on a name. Yet from the moment the child comes out of the womb, parents and family waste no time, and instantly start calling him or her by that name. But when does a person really receive their name? What is the job of the Good Shepherd when it comes to those named ones? Explain how the sequence of naming, calling, and new life/resurrection is displayed at every baptismal font.

How is the binding of Lazarus symbolic of sin? What is symbolized in the unbinding?

What is the ultimate reason for Jesus' coming into this world? How does He do it? Where and how are you made new?

6

Jesus Christ

Lesson Focus

Throughout this series of lessons, there has been an overarching theme of death versus life. They are indeed two forces in complete opposition to each other, and the Scriptures are filled with the antagonism created by the two, which reaches its ultimate climax in the suffering, death, burial, and resurrection of Jesus Christ.

Gospel Focus

Christ, in and of Himself, is the very icon of death and resurrection and the sure and certain hope that life has prevailed!

Prayer

Awake, my heart, with gladness,
See what today is done;
Now, after gloom and sadness,
Comes forth the glorious sun.
My Savior there was laid
Where our bed must be made
When to the realms of light
Our spirit wings its flight.

The foe in triumph shouted
When Christ lay in the tomb;
But lo, he now is routed,
His boast is turned to gloom.
For Christ again is free;
In glorious victory
He who is strong to save
Has triumphed o'er the grave.

Now hell, its prince, the devil,
Of all their pow'r are shorn;
Now I am safe from evil,
And sin I laugh to scorn.
Grim death with all its might
Cannot my soul affright;
It is a pow'rless form,
Howe'er it rave and storm.
("Awake, My Heart, with Gladness,"
LSB 467:1, 2, 4; *LW* 128:1, 2, 4)

Introduction

Throughout the Holy Scriptures, what are the two forces always in opposition?

Why are the four Gospels unique? How can the Gospels be called long introductions to the Passion Narratives?

Luther writes that "all of Scripture . . . is pure Christ" (AE 15:339). He is the substance and source of all Holy Scripture, from Genesis to Revelation. However, the Gospels do find a unique place within the canon (listing of the books of the Bible). All of Scripture is pure Christ, but the four Gospels are the actual words and deeds of the God-man, Jesus Christ. But what is most unique is that these Gospels serve one purpose: to move the listener to the cross and Good Friday, and ultimately to the empty tomb on Easter Sunday. In short, the Gospels are but long introductions to the Passion Narratives, since Jesus Himself says, "The Son of Man must suffer many things and be rejected by the elders and chief priests and scribes, and be killed, and on the third day be raised" (Luke 9:22). There it is! All of Jesus' mission and work summed up in one verse. So yes, "all of Scripture is pure Christ," which always points to His Passion, death, and resurrection.

Bearing Our Grief

Many Christians misunderstand the wrath of God. How is wrath not of God's essence or nature, but a consequence or result of the fall into sin?

In the end, who bears the wrath of God? How does He bear it?

The prophet Isaiah writes of the Passion of Jesus Christ in chapter 53. He says:

> *Surely He has borne our griefs and carried our sorrows; yet we esteemed Him stricken, smitten by God, and afflicted. But He was wounded for our transgressions; He was crushed for our iniquities; upon Him was the chastisement that brought us peace, and with His stripes we are healed.* (53:4–5)

There are several fascinating things about these two verses from the prophet Isaiah. First and foremost, although he is speaking about a future action (i.e., the Passion of Jesus Christ), he writes in the past tense (perfect tense in

Hebrew). Isaiah writes as though the Passion of Jesus is a past action and already completed. This appears to be nonsense, as it would be many years before Jesus would even enter this world. Yet the prophet is so certain that one day the Messiah would come, suffer, and die that, for him, it is already completed.

Moreover, the prophet uses words like "stricken," "smitten," "afflicted," "wounded," and "crushed." These are words of punishment and of bearing the burden of someone's wrath. Yet, of His essence, God is anything but wrathful. Rather, God is love! However, wrath is a consequence of the fall—when man transgresses, someone must pay. That someone is Jesus Christ. It is a complete falsehood or heresy to say that God is wrathful or that He pours out His wrath on human beings even to this day. God is not wrathful of His nature. The only one who bears His consequential wrath is His own dear Son. That is what Christ's Passion is all about. Jesus becomes sin for sinful creation (2 Corinthians 5:21) and receives the wrath that Adam, Eve, and all their children, both past and present, deserve.

True Judgment

Given these texts, what impression do you have of the Last Day? Will it be a "cosmic" day? What do you imagine happening?

Many people are afraid of Judgment Day, but how can you, a Christian, be certain that it will not harm you?

When Jesus said, "It is finished" (John 19:30), what was He talking about? What is finished? Who does Jesus die for? What is the verdict on the world?

Will there be a "Last Day"? When was the true Judgment Day?

Have students read Mark 13:1–13; Matthew 24:15–28; and Matthew 25:1–13.

During the last few Sundays of the Church Year, the texts reflect the cosmic nature of Christ's return. There are talks of wars raging, chaff burning, and virgins scrambling for some extra oil, all in the hope of escaping Judgment Day unscathed. But is that truly the Judgment Day, when the verdict will be handed down by the supreme judge, or is the judgment of God already a done deal?

Just before Jesus becomes lifeless on the cross of Calvary, He utters words that forever change the course of this world. With these words, Jesus Christ shows the world that the true Judgment Day is already taking place. His words from the cross, "It is finished" (John 19:30), do not merely speak of His life. True, Christ's life is finished and He is about to die. But that glorious phrase means so much more. What is finished? Salvation is finished. Judgment is complete. On the cross, Jesus Christ is offered up for the life of the world, a world that is horribly corrupted by sin. Yet, when Jesus hangs on the cross, the world is judged "not guilty." This is the traditional understanding of objective justification in which Christ's death declares to the world that sins are forgiven and all is made new.

Will there be a Judgment Day? Yes, of sorts. There will be a Last Day, when Christ, the chief shepherd and bishop of all souls, will appear and separate the sheep from the goats. Yet the true judgment of the Father is handed out at the cross as His Son dies to give life, and in His "being rejected by God, Jesus' sacrifice is accepted and the end times have come" (Scaer, *Discourses in Matthew*, p. 407).

Making All Things New

Why is Golgotha called "The Place of the Skull"? Whose skull is believed to have been buried under Golgotha?

Read Genesis 3:1–19 (especially v. 19). What was the curse that Adam brought upon all of creation? As sinners, to whom do we belong?

In Jesus' death and resurrection, who is our new head? Read 1 Corinthians 15:21–22. What are the blessings of being under a new head, and no longer under Adam?

The place of Jesus' death is called Golgotha or "The Place of the Skull" (Matthew 27:33; Mark 15:22; Luke 23:33; John 19:17). Many think that the reference to the skull is simply that the place of the crucifixion is a place where many skulls lay. However, there is deeper meaning to the title of this hill. As Arthur Just notes in his commentary, "Jerome suggested that the place called Skull was also the location where Adam was buried. St. John Chrysostom noted that 'according to the belief of some,' Adam was buried under Golgotha" (*Luke 9:51–24:53*, p. 930). Whether or not this is fact, or just pious opinion, the point is very clear: Jesus dies in the place of Adam, as the new and greater Adam.

This image of a substitutionary death is even clearer in icons of the crucifixion. In most, there is a very prominent skull positioned within the hill (Golgotha), under the cross where Jesus is being crucified. The point is that Jesus is the new and greater Adam, in that He reverses the curse brought upon all people by the first Adam. This notion of making wrongs right and reversing curses is what St. Irenaeus (130–202 AD) calls recapitulation. This is a fancy term for bringing things under a new head or master. As Martin Franzmann's hymn declares:

> *In Adam we have all been one,*
> *One huge rebellious man;*
> *We all have fled that evening voice*
> *That sought us when we ran.*
> ("In Adam We Have All Been One," *LSB* 569:1; *LW* 292:1)

As children of Adam, all sinners make up "one huge rebellious man." Yet in Jesus Christ and His bitter substitutionary death, all those who are incorporated into His body through Baptism are also one body. As St. Paul says in 1 Corinthians: "For as by a man came death, by a man has come also the resurrection of the dead. For as in Adam all die, so also in Christ shall all be made alive" (5:21–22). Commenting on St. Paul's juxtaposition of Adam and Christ, Luther says:

> *Paul now poses two different Adams, or two persons, making the first Adam an example or image of the other. The first Adam, he says, is created for natural life. From him we inherit this natural life . . . The other Adam, however, will have and will bestow another life. As you bear the first Adam . . . let me tell you that you will also have the other, the spiritual Adam, when the former ceases to exist.* (AE 28:192)

All who are in Jesus are made alive because in His body and under a new head Christians receive so much more than they originally lost in Adam!

Chief of Sinners and Yet a Lamb

Read or sing "A Lamb Goes Uncomplaining Forth" (*LSB* 438; *TLH* 142). On the cross, whose sins does Jesus bear? Is it wrong to call Jesus the "chief of sinners" as He is hanging on the cross? What is the result of Jesus taking all sin upon Himself?

In what way is Jesus also a lamb?

In what ways has God bound Himself to us, His creation? Was Jesus' death a quick reaction to a problem (sin), or was it always part of the plan?

Jesus' death on the place of the skull is fitting since Jesus is the new and greater Adam. Yet Jesus does not merely die for the sins of Adam. Rather, He dies for Adam's sins, Eve's sins, and the sins of the whole world. It is no wonder that Jesus physically struggles to make His way to the hill of His death and then even to stay alive on the cross. He is not only bearing the weight of the cross, and the shame and mockery that others project upon Him, but He also bears the weight of the world's sin. However, like going to meet the widow's son at Nain, Jesus—

true life—goes to meet death head-on. One of the most amazing hymns for Holy Week is from Paul Gerhardt. In a very terse and poetic fashion, he brings the parishioners to the cross with Jesus and Jesus to the parishioners in the pew. He writes:

A Lamb goes uncomplaining forth,
The guilt of all men bearing;
And laden with the sins of earth,
None else the burden sharing!
Goes patient on, grows weak and faint,
To slaughter led without complaint,
That spotless life to offer;
Bears shame, and stripes, and wounds
and death,
Anguish and mockery, and saith,
"Willing all this I suffer."
("A Lamb Goes Uncomplaining Forth,"
LSB 438:1; *TLH* 142:1)

As John the Baptizer declares, Jesus is "the Lamb of God, who takes away the sin of the world!" (John 1:29). Notice, Christ does not take away bits and pieces, but all the sin of the world. He hangs on the cross as the chief among sinners because there is "none else the burden sharing!" This is how Jesus makes all things new. Sin is what condemns and damns. That is the old way of things or the fallen way. Yet, when Jesus bears the sins of the world, He essentially takes them away and pays for them with His own precious blood. They are no more. They cannot harm anyone. In taking them upon Himself, He makes all things new. Poor sinners who are children of Adam and Eve are now part of the body of Jesus Christ. Sinners who deserve nothing but eternal separation from God in hell are now given access to heaven, and all of it, every last bit of it, is a free gift from Christ!

While bearing the sins of the entire human race, Christ does so in meekness, not even opening His mouth (Isaiah 53:7). Certainly, Jesus can do all things, even prevent His own death. As He says in the Garden of Gethsemane after Simon Peter pulls out his sword to ward off those seeking to take Jesus by force: "Do you think that I cannot appeal to My Father, and He will at once send Me more than twelve legions of angels?" (Matthew 26:53). But that is not the way it is supposed to be. Rather, as Jesus says, "It must be so" (Matthew 26:54).

He is the very Paschal Lamb whom the Father predestines to suffer and die, even before the foundation of the world (see Acts 4:27–28). There is no other way. In creating man and woman, and seeing that they are "very good" (Genesis 1:31), God binds Himself to His creation, and He will not change His mind. He certainly has the power to do as He wills, but, in love, Christ binds Himself to that which He makes, and He therefore must become a man, live as a man, and die as a man. Like the new and greater Isaac being led to the slaughter, He does not and cannot look for a way out, but goes to His death. Jesus Christ, the very Lamb of God who goes uncomplaining forth, is offered up as a burnt offering to the Father in heaven because "it must be so" (Matthew 26:54).

The Unworthy Are Now Worthy

Where does Jesus show His true glory? Discuss how there can be glory in a death.

How is the cosmos altered at the death of Jesus? Compare this with the cosmos being altered at the resurrection of dry bones in Ezekiel 37.

What is the final indication that Jesus is officially dead? Read John 1:14. Explain how Jesus is, in and of Himself, the true tabernacle.

If Jesus is the true tabernacle or tent, then what is the true temple curtain? In the true temple curtain being torn in two, whom do you have access to?

How are the Sacraments seen in the true temple curtain being torn in two?

How is Jesus' death and resurrection now your death and resurrection?

Jesus is the new Adam and the new Isaac because He reverses the curse of Adam by offering Himself upon the altar of the cross. Yet in His death He gives life to the world. Many people, however, feel sad or even angry on Good Friday as they commemorate Jesus' bitter suffering and death. The focus of that day is one of remorse for sin and bitter death. Yet, in that gruesome death, Jesus shows forth His true glory and turns the normal course of this world on its head. His sin is the world's forgiveness, His shame is the world's honor, and His death is the world's life. The cosmic nature of this "great exchange" is made evident by the universal reaction that ensues. As Luke describes, "It was now about the sixth hour, and there was darkness over the whole land until the ninth hour, while the sun's light failed. And the curtain of the temple was torn in two" (Luke 23:44–45). Yes, when God dies on the cross, this earth is forever altered. Following these signs, Jesus "breathed His last" (Luke 23:46). Finally, the three longest hours this world has ever seen are over. All hope appears to be gone.

Often times, a person who is crucified suffers for many hours until the time comes when his legs will need to be broken. This breaking of the legs eliminates the ability to hold oneself up to breathe. Eventually the crucified person suffocates on his own fluid. Yet for Jesus, it does not get this far. Remember the words of the psalmist: "He keeps all His bones; not one of them is broken" (Psalm 34:20). So how do they know Jesus is dead? The true temple curtain is torn in two!

John says Jesus—the Word—became flesh and "dwelt among us" (John 1:14). The word for "dwelt" is more than merely living in a certain locale. It literally means to "tabernacle" or "tent" (*skanase*) among us. God's name, and with that His presence, is always found in the temple (see 1 Kings 9:3: "I have consecrated this house that you have built, by putting My name there forever."). However, there is a dramatic shift in God's presence when the angel comes to Mary and speaks those life-giving words: "The Holy Spirit will come upon you, and the power of the Most High will overshadow you; therefore the child to be born will be called holy—the Son of God" (Luke 1:35). Just as the waiting father comes down the hill to meet his delinquent child in the parable of the prodigal son (Luke 15:11–32), so now has the presence of God Himself come down from heaven to meet His fallen, delinquent children. With the incarnation, there is a shift in God's presence, and Jesus Christ as the new "tabernacle" is the place where the Most High dwells.

Therefore, it is no coincidence that John pays particular attention to the sword piercing Jesus' flesh. He says: "But when they came to Jesus and saw that He was already dead, they did not break His legs. But one of the soldiers pierced His side with a spear, and at once there came out blood and water" (John 19:33–34). No broken legs, just the veil of His flesh torn in two. Jesus is the new and greater tabernacle (or temple), and the new and greater veil is rent asunder, spewing forth blood and water. With a close reading of John's Gospel, one will notice that there is no official institution of the Sacraments by Jesus. Where are they then? They are where God is, in the tabernacle of Jesus' body. When blood and water gush forth, they show to all that from Jesus comes both the Holy Supper and Holy Baptism. True access to God does not occur by entering into a temple that no longer has a curtain restricting people from entering the Holy of Holies. No, the body of Jesus is true entrance to God. It is when a person is incorporated into that precious body through the waters of Holy Baptism, and nourished on the way with the flesh and blood of Jesus, that he has true access to the Most High.

A Return to the Manger

Why is it necessary that Jesus be brought down from the cross?

Joseph of Arimathea is "looking for the kingdom of God" (Mark 15:43). Does he find it?

Discuss how Jesus' descent from the cross is actually a return to the nativity. What is the significance of Jesus being wrapped in "linen cloths" (John 19:40)?

Why was Jesus born?

The bitter suffering and death of the Lamb are now over and Jesus Christ, God in the flesh, is dead. It is almost sundown though, and His body needs to be removed. As Deuteronomy 21:22–23 states:

And if a man has committed a crime punishable by death and he is put to death, and you hang him on a tree, his body shall not remain all night on the tree, but you shall bury him the same day, for a hanged man is cursed by God. You shall not defile your land that the LORD your God is giving you for an inheritance.

It is a matter of the Law that Jesus come down from the tree, and all of the Gospels name Joseph of Arimathea as the key player in Jesus' burial. One fascinating note that Mark and Luke make is that this Joseph of Arimathea is "looking for the kingdom of God" (Mark 15:43; see also Luke 23:51). Remember back to the story of Lazarus and Jesus' statement that the glory of God is to be seen in His raising Lazarus from the dead (John 11:40). Why? God's glory is seen in His suffering, death, and resurrection, and the account of Lazarus is but a foretaste of the things to come. Jesus' Passion and death are two of those good things, and wherever the glory of God is, there is His kingdom.

The kingdom of God is Jesus Christ, and people enter it by entering into Jesus' body through Baptism (see John 3:5 and His discussion with Nicodemus, who also happens to be present in the burial account of John [19:39]). But that kingdom, Jesus, begins to come to fruition in the action that solidifies His purpose, His own bitter suffering and death.

Just explains:

Luke suggests to the hearer that already now a major stage in the kingdom's coming has taken place with the death of Jesus. Next, Jesus will take His Sabbath rest in the tomb, and then on the third day He shall bring His kingdom's reign to all creation when He rises from the dead. Probably none of the faithful, including Joseph, had envisioned the kingdom's imminent coming in quite these terms. (*Just*, p. 952)

The one who is looking for the kingdom of God is actually holding Him in his arms and transporting Him to his own tomb. The kingdom of God, which comes down from heaven in the incarnation, now descends from the cross, but ironically, here at what appears to be the end, there is a return to the beginning of the story. "So they took the body of Jesus and bound it in linen cloths" (John 19:40). This is the sign of death, but it is also the sign of life and of the presence of the kingdom of God. It is a sign for Joseph of Arimathea, just as much as it is a sign for the shepherds looking for the newborn king.

Fear not, for behold, I bring you good news of great joy that will be for all the people. For unto you is born this day in the city of David a Savior, who is Christ the Lord. And this will be a sign for you: you will find a baby wrapped in swaddling cloths and lying in a manger. (Luke 2:10–12)

This text, with "killed" for "born" and "man" for "baby," could very easily be spoken to Joseph of Arimathea as he looks to bury Jesus Christ. Certainly, Jesus was born to die! Therefore, it is indeed "good news" that Christ, the Paschal Lamb, is slain for the sins of the world. It is appropriate, however, that His body receives the proper attention on the day of preparation.

Preparing and Burying—Jonah Fulfilled!

Review the resurrection of Jonah. Read Matthew 12:40. What are the connections between Jonah and Jesus?

As the followers of Jesus were observing their own Sabbath rest, what were some of the things they must have been thinking? Do you think hope was gone?

The entire Passover and exodus stories find their fulfillment in the suffering, death, and resurrection of Jesus Christ. They are meant to be read in light of Jesus Christ. "All of Scripture . . . is pure Christ" since every person, place, and thing is meant to point the hearer to Jesus. He is both the substance and the goal of all Scripture. This preparation of the Lamb for burial is "the end of this climactic day in salvation history" (*Just*, p. 953) and the salvific act is nearing its completion as Jesus is placed in the tomb. Once again, Just says:

> *At the beginning of this Day of Preparation God prepared Jesus' body for death by providing Passover food to sustain Him during His "exodus" (9:31). At the close of this day, God ensures that Jesus' same body, now dead, is prepared for burial and Sabbath rest. From now on, this Day of Preparation will be called Good Friday, because here God prepared the greatest good for His creation: renewal, restoration, and re-creation.* (*Just*, p. 953)

"For just as Jonah was three days and three nights in the belly of the great fish, so will the Son of Man be three days and three nights in the heart of the earth" (Matthew 12:40), says Jesus. Jonah finds his grave to be a watery one, and Jesus' is hewn out of a rock. Yet the mere fact that they are buried presupposes a resurrection. Granted, these followers of Jesus may not fully get it. They observe their own Sabbath rests on Saturday, and make their way to the tomb on the first day of the week to visit the corpse. Little do they know that the first day is really the eighth day, or the day of the new creation, and they will find that Jesus is not dead—but alive!

All Things New!

What was the significance of the seventh day? Why is the seventh day no longer the final day? On what day does Christ rise from the dead? How is the day of the resurrection the eighth day?

What does the number eight stand for? How does Jesus, in His death and resurrection, make all things new?

Why is it significant that Christ is seen pulling Adam and Eve up from their graves?

How does this bring out the theology of the new creation?

All four of the Gospels give a time reference to the account of the resurrection of Jesus Christ. Christ's death is on Good Friday, His rest in the tomb on Holy Saturday, and now it is Sunday, or the first day of the week. The number seven is the number of completion, since the creation account lasts seven days, with God's rest on Saturday, the day of the Sabbath. Yet that complete creation soon becomes incomplete and corruptible as it is ridden with sin. It is a fallen creation that is destined for eternal death. It is in need of redemption and new life. It needs to be re-created!

Jesus' resurrection on the first day of the week takes the hearer one day further than the old creation, where God rests on Day 7. This is the next day, or the eighth day, if you will. God is not starting over again, but He is taking His old creation and making it new, or re-creating it. This small detail, "the first day of the week" (Matthew 28:1; Mark 16:2; Luke 24:1; John 20:1) is at the heart and soul of the resurrection of Jesus Christ. It is not only a marker of time, but it is a marker of salvation. Unless Jesus rises from the dead, creation is still old and deteriorating. Jesus rises from the dead on the eighth day, or the day of the new creation, because in Him, all things are made new.

The theology of new creation is clearly seen in various icons of the resurrection of Jesus Christ. Most take the usual form of Jesus coming out of the tomb, with his hands reaching out for two people who are standing up out of their caskets. Theologically, it does not get any richer than this! Why? In Jesus' resurrection, Christ sets free all the prisoners of sin, death, and the devil. His resurrection liberates the captives, and gives new life to all who are dead in sin and transgressions. In the icons of the resurrection, all of creation, bound up in sin, is represented by two figures: Adam and Eve. Yes, it is Adam and Eve, who fell in the old creation and found the grave as their resting place, who are being pulled up out of the caskets by the resurrected Christ. In His death, they have life. In fact, in His death, all people have new life!

Eighth Day—Forever!

How can you say that you always live in the eighth day?

Will your new life in Jesus Christ ever end?

What day is today? How does Jesus permeate and continue to remake His creation?

Jesus' resurrection on the eighth day rings in the new creation. All things are made new as Jesus dies and rises again. Although earthly days will certainly come and go, theologically, Jesus' re-creating resurrection is always a reality. In other words, there is no other day except the eighth day. All Christians who are baptized into Jesus and made partakers of His death and resurrection will forever live in the ongoing eighth day. With Jesus, it is always new creation because it is always about forgiveness, life, and salvation. Yes, sin and death still haunt the children of God, but there is a hope that surpasses all things, a hope of the resurrection of all flesh and life eternal with Christ. A hope of entering the Garden of Eden made new, the land of the new creation, that is, heaven itself! Luther says of this day of the new creation:

> *The eighth day signifies the future life; for Christ rested in the sepulcher on the Sabbath, that is, during the entire seventh day, but rose again on the day which follows the Sabbath, which is the eighth day and the beginning of a new week, and after it no other day is counted. For through His death Christ brought to a close the weeks of time and on the eighth day entered into a different kind of life, in which days are no longer counted but there is one eternal day without the alternations of night. . . . For the rising Christ is no longer subject to days, months, weeks, or any number of days; He is in a new and eternal life. The beginning of this life is perceived and reckoned, but there is no end.*
> (AE *3:141*)

Sunday, the eighth day and the day of the resurrection, now permeates all days. There will never be another re-creation or another day; this is it. The eighth day reigns forever because on the cross Jesus said, "It is finished" (John 19:30). What is finished? Salvation is finished. Sins are forgiven. With the empty tomb, "Jesus lives! The victory's won!" (*LSB* 490; *LW* 139) and all things are made new. Jesus does not rise from the grave to lock Himself in heaven. Rather, He rises from the dead that He might go into all the world and bring with Him the new creation. Yes, Jesus spreads and permeates this creation through the confession of witnesses, proclamation of the Holy Gospel, and delivery of His sacramental gifts, and He will continue to do so until the end of time. Eighth day forever!

Fear Not!

Read the resurrection accounts from the four Gospels. Imagine going to the tomb and finding it empty. What would have been your reaction? What would you have seen? What would you have heard? What would you have thought?

What is the cause of fear? How did the empty tomb cause fear? How is fear sinful?

Why did the angel tell those fearful ones to "not fear"?

Jesus' resurrection is completely unexpected. Although the apostles and followers of Jesus should know that He will rise on the third day, they are caught off guard when He actually does. Luke says that Mary Magdalene, Joanna, Mary the mother of James, and the other women "were frightened" (Luke 24:5) at the appearance of the empty tomb and the two men in "dazzling apparel" (Luke 24:4). Matthew records that it is the guards at the tomb, and probably Mary Magdalene and the other Mary as well, who are afraid at the appearance of the angel (Matthew 28:4). Why are they afraid? They are afraid because the resurrection of Jesus and appearance of angels is not what they originally expected. They thought Jesus was dead and now they find His tomb empty. However, that does not excuse their fear. Fear, as Norman Nagel once preached, "is self-regarding" (*Selected Sermons*, p. 76). In other words, fear is always concerned with one's self, and therefore is always self-centered and sinful.

Yet what is more remarkable is what the angel says to those frightened ones: "Do not be afraid" (Matthew 28:5). The words spoken by the angel in the original Greek (*may fo-bisthey*) are the same words the angel Gabriel speaks to the Virgin Mary at the announcement (annunciation) of Jesus' birth, once again bringing His life full-circle. Jesus became a man to die and rise again. Although the frightened ones are caught in fearful sin, the angel utters words of absolution, "Do not be afraid" or "Do not sin" because Jesus "is not here, for He has risen, as He said" (Matthew 28:6). There is no need for worry or fear. There is no need to be self-centered or self-serving. Just rejoice and be glad, for Christ is risen! Sins are forgiven and all of creation has hope.

He's No Ghost

Jesus died as a man, but did He rise as a ghost or spirit?

If Jesus had not risen with flesh and blood as a man, would there be a Lord's Supper? How is the Lord's Supper at the heart of the new creation?

What does Jesus bring with Him to the altar? How are you changed by feasting on the flesh and body of Jesus?

In all of the Gospels except Mark, Jesus appears to individuals as a fleshly man, and not merely as a ghost or spirit. The reason for Mark's omission is easily understood in that Mark is using Matthew's Gospel as his source, and need not re-tell all the details of that first Gospel. Needless to say, it is clear from the other Gospels that Jesus rose from the dead with a body. In Matthew's Gospel, the women take hold of His feet (Matthew 28:9); in Luke's Gospel, Jesus appears to the two on the Emmaus road and also to all the disciples and eats with them (Luke 24:13–43); and in John's Gospel there is the great scene where the unbelieving Thomas gets the chance to put his fingers in Jesus' hand and thrust his hand into Jesus' side (John 20:24–29). All of this is just evidence of the fact that Jesus rose from the dead as a man, with flesh and blood, and continues to live as such to this day.

Had Jesus risen from the dead as a mere spirit, He would not have re-created all things. Rather, Jesus rises from the dead with a resurrected, perfect body, and it is that perfected flesh and blood that Jesus gives to His bride, the Church, in the Lord's Supper. He need not come to the altars of His Church by way of locked doors, but He now comes by His own life-giving word. "Take, eat; this is My body. . . Drink of it, all of you, for this is My blood of the covenant" (Matthew 26:26–28). Yes, Jesus comes to the holy altar with the same body and blood that enters the room full of disciples, that the women touch as He appears to them, and that Mary Magdalene longs to cling to as He calls her by name. In this gracious act, Jesus joins His Church to His own flesh and blood in the Holy Supper, and by it continually makes things new. Yes, the Lord's Supper, that most holy of meals, is at the heart and soul of the new creation.

Since Christ brings all that He is and all that He has to the altar, Christians can rejoice in being joined to Him in a physical, tangible, life-restoring way. Luther says in his work on the Lord's Supper:

> *If we eat Him spiritually through the Word, He abides in us spiritually in our soul; if one eats Him physically, He abides in us physically and we in Him. As we eat Him, He abides in us and we in Him. For He is not digested or transformed but ceaselessly He transforms us, our soul into righteousness, our body into immortality. So the ancient fathers spoke of the physical eating.* (AE 37:132)

No, Jesus is not locked in heaven, and no, a person does not need to ascend to Him and feast upon Him only spiritually. Rather, Jesus rises and ascends with His body, blood, soul, and divinity, and He brings all of that, every last bit of it, to the altar. He abides in those who eat and drink, and they in Him, all with the assurance of sins forgiven, a perfect, resurrected body like Jesus, and life eternal with Him! New creations to be sure!

Resurrected with Christ

Where is Christ's resurrection applied and given to you?

What was an Early Church Easter Vigil like? What would you have seen? What would you have heard? What would you have smelled?

How does the awe-inspiring Easter Vigil help to bring out the importance of the resurrection of Jesus and Holy Baptism?

Why is an eight-sided font particularly appropriate for Baptism?

What happens in the waters of Holy Baptism? Is anything killed? What emerges from those waters?

Into whom are people baptized? In Him, what do people receive?

The resurrection is the highest feast in the Church Year. However, it does not mean anything unless it is applied to dead sinners who are in need of new life. How is the resurrection of Jesus Christ given to those in such need? It all happens at the font of new life, the font of resurrection, the font of Holy Baptism. Too often today, it is hard to recognize the significance of this Sacrament. In fact, many neglect this gift, not seeing the true blessings it bestows. Moreover, many see it as a mere entrance into the Church (which it certainly is, but only in part) and not an actual dying and rising again. In the Early Church, however, and even in some churches today, the imagery of death and resurrection are very clear.

In the Early Church, Baptisms were often reserved for the great Vigil of Easter, or Holy Saturday. After sundown on Saturday, late in the night and early into the morning on Sunday, Christians and those preparing for Baptism (Catechumens) would gather for hours (hence, "vigil") of prayer and singing until the climax of the service, the Baptisms. The catechumens would gather in the darkness and chill of the spring night/morning, and together they would enter into the warmth and glow of a baptistery lit with candles and smelling of incense. That baptistery was fertile ground, where the Spirit would give birth to new Christians in the womb of the holy font (the Church is a loving mother, and her womb is that baptismal font). It was reminiscent of the Garden of Eden, where creation was perfect and truly considered paradise. After making this transition from darkness to light, the catechumens would enter into the holy font, usually made of eight sides. They would actually walk down into the font, be submerged under the water as a sign that they were drowning and killing their sinful nature (Old Adam as Luther's Small Catechism calls it), and then walk up and out the other side as a new creation. From the womb of the font, those catechumens were now Christians who had been reborn in the waters of Baptism. For the newly baptized, those words of Jesus to Nicodemus truly came to light:

> *Jesus answered him, "Truly, truly, I say to you, unless one is born again he cannot see the kingdom of God." Nicodemus said to Him, "How can a man be born when he is old? Can he enter a second time into his mother's womb and be born?" Jesus answered, "Truly, truly, I say to you, unless one is born of water and the Spirit, he cannot enter the kingdom of God."* (John 3:3–5)

Baptism is indeed new birth and a resurrection from death to sin. It is fitting, then, that baptismal fonts have eight sides, as this Holy Sacrament is actually bringing forth a new creation. Sinners who pass through those sacred waters emerge as new creations because of the one into whom they are now incorporated. As St. Paul says in Romans 6:

> *Do you not know that all of us who have been baptized into Christ Jesus were baptized into His death? We were buried therefore with Him by Baptism into death, in order that, just as Christ was raised from the dead by the glory of the Father, we too might walk in newness of life.* (vv. 3–4)

Baptism is a death, burial, and resurrection, not alone, but "into Christ Jesus." The baptized are new creations because they reside in the body of Christ, who rose victorious in a perfected, eighth-day body. He brings in the new creation that will never end, and Christians partake of that as they are incorporated into Him through the font.

Conclusion

Death and resurrection are two forces completely at odds with one another. Death seeks to destroy and resurrection seeks to give eternal life. In His bitter passion and death and victorious resurrection, Jesus—who is life Himself—destroys death forever. Death no longer has dominion. Death no longer can haunt the Christian. As St. Paul declares, "'Death is swallowed up in victory.' 'O death, where is your victory? O death where is your sting?'" (1 Corinthians 15:54–55). And so it is! Death no longer has dominion, and though all people die, there is a sure and certain hope of the resurrection and life eternal for all Christians who are baptized into Jesus' resurrected, fleshly body!

Prayer

Water, blood, and Spirit crying,
By their witness testifying
To the One whose death defying
Life has come, with life for all.

In a wat'ry grave are buried
All our sins that Jesus carried;
Christ, the Ark of Life, has ferried
Us across death's raging flood.

Dark the way, yet Christ precedes us,
Past the scowl of death He leads us;
Spreads a Table where He feeds us
With His body and His blood.

Though around us death is seething,
God, His two-edged sword unsheathing,
By His Spirit life is breathing
Through the living, active Word.

Spirit, water, blood entreating,
Working faith and its completing
In the One whose death-defeating
Life has come, with life for all.
("Water, Blood, and Spirit Crying," *LSB* 597)

6

JESUS CHRIST

Introduction

Throughout the Holy Scriptures, what are the two forces always in opposition?

Why are the four Gospels unique? How can the Gospels be called long introductions to the Passion Narratives?

Bearing Our Grief

Many Christians misunderstand the wrath of God. How is wrath not of God's essence or nature, but a consequence or result of the fall into sin?

In the end, who bears the wrath of God? How does He bear it?

True Judgment

Read the following:
Mark 13:1–13
Matthew 24:15–28
Matthew 25:1–13
Given these texts, what impression do you have of the Last Day? Will it be a "cosmic" day? What do you imagine happening?

Many people are afraid of Judgment Day, but how can you, a Christian, be certain that it will not harm you?

When Jesus said, "It is finished" (**John 19:30**), what was He talking about? What is finished? Who does Jesus die for? What is the verdict on the world?

Will there be a "Last Day"? When was the true Judgment Day?

Making All Things New

Why is Golgotha called "The Place of the Skull"? Whose skull is believed to have been buried under Golgotha?

Read **Genesis 3:1–19** (especially **v. 19**). What was the curse that Adam brought upon all of creation? As sinners, to whom do we belong?

In Jesus' death and resurrection, who is our new head? Read **1 Corinthians 15:21–22**. What are the blessings of being under a new head, and no longer under Adam?

Chief of Sinners and Yet a Lamb

Read or sing "A Lamb Goes Uncomplaining Forth" (*LSB* 438; *TLH* 142). On the cross, whose sins does Jesus bear? Is it wrong to call Jesus the "chief of sinners" as He is hanging on the cross? What is the result of Jesus taking all sin upon Himself?

In what way is Jesus also a lamb?

In what ways has God bound Himself to us, His creation? Was Jesus' death a quick reaction to a problem (sin), or was it always part of the plan?

The Unworthy Are Now Worthy

Where does Jesus show His true glory? Discuss how there can be glory in a death.

How is the cosmos altered at the death of Jesus? Compare this with the cosmos being altered at the resurrection of dry bones in **Ezekiel 37**.

What is the final indication that Jesus is officially dead? Read **John 1:14**. Explain how Jesus is, in and of Himself, the true tabernacle.

If Jesus is the true tabernacle or tent, then what is the true temple curtain? In the true temple curtain being torn in two, whom do you have access to?

How are the Sacraments seen in the true temple curtain being torn in two?

How is Jesus' death and resurrection now your death and resurrection?

A Return to the Manger

Why is it necessary that Jesus be brought down from the cross?

Joseph of Arimathea is "looking for the kingdom of God" (**Mark 15:43**). Does he find it?

Discuss how Jesus' descent from the cross is actually a return to the nativity. What is the significance of Jesus being wrapped in "linen cloths" (**John 19:40**)?

Why was Jesus born?

Preparing and Burying—Jonah Fulfilled!

Review the resurrection of Jonah. Read **Matthew 12:40**. What are the connections between Jonah and Jesus?

As the followers of Jesus were observing their own Sabbath rest, what were some of the things they must have been thinking? Do you think hope was gone?

All Things New!

What was the significance of the seventh day? Why is the seventh day no longer the final day? On what day does Christ rise from the dead? How is the day of the resurrection the eighth day?

What does the number eight stand for? How does Jesus, in His death and resurrection, make all things new?

Why is it significant that Christ is seen pulling Adam and Eve up from their graves?

How does this bring out the theology of the new creation?

Eighth Day—Forever!

How can you say that you always live in the eighth day?

Will your new life in Jesus Christ ever end?

What day is today? How does Jesus permeate and continue to remake His creation?

Fear Not!

Read the resurrection accounts from the four Gospels. Imagine going to the tomb and finding it empty. What would have been your reaction? What would you have seen? What would you have heard? What would you have thought?

What is the cause of fear? How did the empty tomb cause fear? How is fear sinful?

Why did the angel tell those fearful ones to "not fear"?

He's No Ghost

Jesus died as a man, but did He rise as a ghost or spirit?

If Jesus had not risen with flesh and blood as a man, would there be a Lord's Supper? How is the Lord's Supper at the heart of the new creation?

What does Jesus bring with Him to the altar? How are you changed by feasting on the flesh and body of Jesus?

Resurrected with Christ

Where is Christ's resurrection applied and given to you?

What was an Early Church Easter Vigil like? What would you have seen? What would you have heard? What would you have smelled? How does the awe-inspiring Easter Vigil help to bring out the importance of the resurrection of Jesus and Holy Baptism?

Why is an eight-sided font particularly appropriate for Baptism?

What happens in the waters of Holy Baptism? Is anything killed? What emerges from those waters?

Into whom are people baptized? In Him, what do people receive?